BUYING PROFESSIONAL SERVICES

OTHER ECONOMIST BOOKS

Guide to Analysing Companies
Guide to Business Modelling
Guide to Business Planning
Guide to Economic Indicators
Guide to the European Union
Guide to Financial Management
Guide to Financial Markets
Guide to Hedge Funds
Guide to Investment Strategy
Guide to Management Ideas and Gurus
Guide to Organisation Design
Guide to Project Management
Guide to Supply Chain Management
Numbers Guide
Style Guide

Book of Obituaries
Brands and Branding
Business Consulting
The City
Coaching and Mentoring
Dealing with Financial Risk
Doing Business in China
Economics
Emerging Markets
The Future of Technology
Headhunters and How to Use Them
Mapping the Markets
Marketing
Organisation Culture
Successful Strategy Execution
The World of Business

Directors: an A–Z Guide
Economics: an A–Z Guide
Investment: an A–Z Guide
Negotiation: an A–Z Guide

Pocket World in Figures

The
Economist

BUYING PROFESSIONAL SERVICES

How to get value for money from consultants
and other professional services providers

Fiona Czerniawska and **Peter Smith**

THE ECONOMIST IN ASSOCIATION WITH
PROFILE BOOKS LTD

Published by Profile Books Ltd
3A Exmouth House, Pine Street, London EC1R 0JH
www.profilebooks.com

Typeset in EcoType by MacGuru Ltd
info@macguru.org.uk

Printed in Great Britain by
Clays, Bungay, Suffolk

A CIP catalogue record for this book is available
from the British Library

ISBN 978 1 84668 325 1

The paper this book is printed on is certified by the © 1996 Forest Stewardship
Council A.C. (FSC). It is ancient-forest friendly. The printer holds FSC chain of custody
SGS-COC-2061

FSC
Mixed Sources
Product group from well-managed
forests and other controlled sources
Cert no. SGS-COC-2061
www.fsc.org
© 1996 Forest Stewardship Council

Contents

Acknowledgements

W e would like to thank everyone who contributed to this book, both directly and indirectly. In particular, we are grateful to all our interviewees, who gave their time and material generously. We would also like to thank everyone we have worked with over the years in this field, whose own knowledge and experience we have tried to capture here, and Stephen Brough and Penny Williams at Profile Books, whose input throughout has been invaluable and much appreciated.

We hope that readers find the book helpful and we welcome feedback from users and providers of professional services. You can contact us via our websites (which include our email addresses):

http://www.sourceforconsulting.com/
http://blog.procurement-excellence.com/

Fiona Czerniawska
Peter Smith
June 2010

Introduction

Bought properly, professional services can help organisations grow, meet their objectives, and operate efficiently and ethically. Expenditure on such services can have a return of tens or even hundreds of times its cost.

But the converse also applies. Much of the expenditure on professional services is wasted or, even worse, has a negative impact, which can result in losses many times the cost of the services in the first place. Although 86% of executives who had used consultants said they were either satisfied or very satisfied with the work consultants had done (according to an independent survey carried out by the Management Consultancies Association in 2006), many feel they do not obtain value for money. Problems are sometimes the result of the incompetence or greed of the professional firms. However, in most cases they can be attributed to poor performance somewhere in the purchasing and management process, such as a confused specification of the requirement, lazy or ill-informed supplier selection, a weak or unbalanced contract, or ineffective contract or supplier management.

It is not easy to buy professional services because of their intangibility and the lack of objective information to support purchasing decisions; and the seniority of those involved on both the supplier and the client side presents challenges to purchasing departments because of the high-level relationships they entail. All of this suggests that substantial expertise is needed to buy professional services well and to understand the ability of the supply side to deliver what is required. It also suggests that effective tools, techniques and approaches will be critical and that, while some of these may well be common to other areas of purchasing, others will be specific to the particular challenges involved in commissioning professional services. It is also clear that although professional purchasing has a role to play, the involvement of internal stakeholders in the purchasing and supplier management process is crucial.

The purpose of this book is to help organisations purchase professional services more efficiently, more effectively and in a way that brings value and benefits to all the parties involved.

The purchasing function

Buying goods and services is a fundamental function of any organisation, but its importance has only comparatively recently been recognised. Harvard University offered a course on purchasing as early as 1917, partly in recognition of the role it played in the development of America's railways. But until the 1960s, except where managers took charge of their own purchasing, those who did the job were often people in clerical roles typically working in manufacturing organisations. Elsewhere, purchasing was done by whichever manager or budget holder required the goods or services in question. However, since the 1960s purchasing has developed as a business function in its own right, largely in recognition of the impact it can have on performance.

Most large organisations, whether public or private, now spend between 40% and 60% of their income on buying goods and services. If half an organisation's revenue is going to suppliers, making sure that the right amount of money is spent, and that it is spent well, is fundamental to the organisation's success.

Historically, organisations focused most of their efforts on improving their purchase of goods, but two factors have shifted their attention to the way in which they buy services.

First, they are less vertically integrated. No organisation today would follow Henry Ford's ideas and have all the functions it needed in-house. Focusing on "core" activities and buying in "non-core" services is widely accepted by public and private organisations alike. In its broadest sense, outsourcing involves converting internal staff and other costs into external goods and services, to be purchased when required.

Second, over the past few decades there has been growth in new types of services; for example, one of the three largest areas of expenditure for police forces in most developed countries is now forensic services. Similarly, audit and law firms have involved themselves in a far greater range of activities, as have consulting firms.

As organisations came to rely and spend more on outside services, it became increasingly important to purchase them effectively. Ironically, purchasing executives, perhaps deterred by budget holders who wanted to retain control of professional services purchasing decisions, took their time to move into this area, and when they did, they found it difficult. When the purchasing director of a major bank suggested that his team could help negotiate the fees paid to investment bankers, the suggestion was met with a firm "Don't push your luck" from the chief financial officer.

The purchasing process

Whatever term is used – purchasing, procurement, supply chain management and so on – what matters is the end-to-end process by which one organisation buys goods and services from others. That process involves defining the need in terms of quantity and specification; researching the market or suppliers; choosing suppliers; negotiating and forming a contract; and then managing the supplier to get what has been agreed (Figure 1). It also includes all the administrative functions: order processing, delivery and receipt, invoicing, payment and recording.

With some exceptions, the principles this book outlines for buying professional services can be applied to any area of expenditure. For example, it is always important to:

- understand the market and suppliers;
- have effective processes for selecting the right suppliers;
- make sure that contracts are appropriate;
- manage the contract and the supplier relationship effectively so that suppliers meet their obligations.

However, purchasing executives often mistakenly assume that all areas of expenditure can be handled in the same way. With professional services this is not so because:

- end-users, many of whom may be in senior positions, have an important role to play in their purchase;
- the impact of professional services may be many times the amount paid out in fees;
- the value of most professional services lies in the extent to which they have been tailored to the specific needs of an organisation;
- the people who decide whether or not to hire a professional firm find it difficult to obtain information on which to base their decision.

It is clear that purchasing departments and staff are gaining much greater influence in the buying of professional services. Although the additional discipline they often bring is in many ways positive, the comments from senior budget holders in this book make it clear that this trend could easily reverse. If purchasing people do not appreciate internal client needs, if they do not make the effort to understand the market, suppliers and how the industries in question work, they could find that

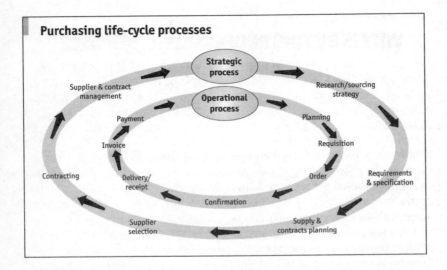

Purchasing life-cycle processes

- Strategic process
- Operational process
- Supplier & contract management
- Research/sourcing strategy
- Payment
- Planning
- Invoice
- Requisition
- Contracting
- Delivery/receipt
- Order
- Requirements & specification
- Confirmation
- Supplier selection
- Supply & contracts planning

they are again marginalised. Users and senior executives will decide that purchasing is adding little value and is a barrier to doing business effectively in a fast-changing and dynamic world. Purchasers need to continually raise their game or risk forfeiting the influence they have gained over recent years.

This book aims to help those involved in all aspects of buying professional services – from the strategic context, through practical advice on the process to long-term supplier management – make better decisions. Bought wisely and in a disciplined way, professional services can play a crucial role in helping organisations manage their performance, protect their interests and pursue their strategic goals. Bought poorly, they can cost an organisation far more than the fees paid. When things go wrong, it is often tempting to blame the suppliers, but the fault usually lies as much, if not more, on the buyer's side. As Niccolò Machiavelli rightly observed in *The Prince*: "Good advice depends on the shrewdness of the prince who seeks it."

PART 1
WHY IS BUYING PROFESSIONAL SERVICES DIFFERENT?

This book is predicated on the belief that buying professional services is substantially different from buying products and even other types of service.

All professional services are knowledge-based and are, at least to some degree, tailored to suit the needs of the people buying them. However, they range from the highly intangible and difficult to measure to those with a clear and concrete output. They vary, too, in the time they take to be carried out and produce results: some in short projects, others over years. There is demand for them because professional services firms employ people with scarce, specialist skills, who are able to think clearly and rigorously about particular issues and who may be able to help get things done.

But they are not easy to buy. Success depends on how effective the working relationship is between the client and professional adviser, something that is hard to gauge in advance. The people involved on both sides are typically smart and senior, and may not welcome interference in the buying process. However, the value an organisation expects to derive from its professional advisers is always much higher than the fees it pays. In short, the difficulties faced when buying professional services are ones for which conventional procurement training provides little guidance.

1 The professional services sector

The rise of the professional services industry

Professional services is big business. In 2008, the sectors on which this book focuses – legal services, management and IT consulting, and accounting and financial advisory – are together estimated to have been worth around $1.2 trillion, larger than Mexico's GDP and about the same size as India's.

Not surprisingly, as a result of its growth and size, the professional services industry has attracted greater scrutiny and, increasingly, criticism. In January 2010, the *Guardian* reported:

> Investment bankers, lawyers, accountants and PR advisers racked up fees at a rate of more than £2m a day during the acrimonious £12 billion battle for control of Cadbury in the latest sign that it is business as usual in the City, barely 15 months after the fall of Lehman Brothers brought the financial system to the brink of collapse.

Not long before, in December 2009, the *Times* reported that influential shareholders in City institutions were demanding a competition enquiry into the fees charged by investment banks in takeover deals. One investor is reported as saying:

> It is egregious. The pensions and savings of our customers are being used to pay ludicrous investment banking fees, which are leading to supernormal profits at the banks and then leaving through the door as excessive bonuses.

In January 2010, *The Economist*'s target was the government's use of consultants:

> Consultants are nothing if not ingenious in getting their feet on the fender. The Obama administration looked like a perfect mark when it came to Washington, DC, on a wave of hope and hype (Mr Obama even created the new job of "chief performance officer"). Monitor Group, based in Boston, has signed up Libya's Colonel

Qaddafi as a client. McKinsey actually scented an opportunity in the credit crunch: an article in the consultancy's house magazine urged that governments needed to go in for "whole-government transformation" if they were to cope with the mess.

Governments are not alone: a 2006 report into the UK government's use of consultants by the National Audit Office suggested that at least 3% of a private-sector company's costs go on professional services.

The legal services sector

When, in 2008, *The Lawyer* introduced its "Sweet Sixteen" (see Table 1.1) – the transatlantic law firms it thought had the profits, clients, international coverage and brand to justifiably claim to be the world's leading law firms – it could not have predicted that the following year would have been the "darkest days seen by the top global law firms since the Great Depression". Allen & Overy cut its staff by 9%; Clifford Chance endured three rounds of lay-offs in the United States; Law Shucks, a legal-industry blog, counted 218 reports of lay-offs at 138 big firms. "It is definitely not 'business as usual'," commented Walt Smith, managing partner of Baker Botts, towards the end of 2009.

But law firms and observers of them expect growth in legal services to return as the world economy recovers and the level of mergers and acquisitions picks up. Datamonitor, a research firm, estimates that the global legal services market (covering commercial, criminal, legal aid, insolvency, labour/industrial, family and taxation law) was worth around $580 billion in 2008 and expects it to rise to more than $700 billion by 2013. The Americas accounted for just over half the market in 2008, and Europe for just over one-third. The short-term and long-term focus will, however, be on profits: culling partner and associate numbers, greater use of technology and operational efficiencies are all likely to increase revenue per lawyer over the next five years (Table 1.2).

Management and IT consulting

The consulting industry breaks almost cleanly down the middle. Just under half the market comes from traditional management consulting, covering consulting in operations management, human resources and strategy and general business advisory services: this was worth just over $141 billion in 2008 (Figure 1.1). Just over half was the IT consulting industry, at $163 billion. Despite recent growth in consulting in countries such as India and China, North America still accounts for 45% of the total (Figure 1.2).

Table 1.1 *The Lawyer's "Sweet Sixteen"*

Firm	Estimated no. of staff
Allen & Overy	5,000
Clifford Chance	3,600
Clearly Gottlieb Steen & Hamilton	1,100
Cravath Swaine & Moore	–
Debevoise & Plimpton	700
Davis Polk & Wardwell	750
Freshfields Bruckhaus Deringer	2,400
Kirkland & Ellis	1,500
Latham & Watkins	2,000
Linklaters	5,100
Simpson Thacher & Bartlett	800
Skadden Arps Slate Meagher & Flom	2,000
Slaughter and May	770
Sullivan & Cromwell	800
Wachtell Lipton Rosen & Katz	–
Weil Gotshal & Manges	1,200

Sources: Firms' websites; authors' estimates

Beyond top-level service and geography, segmenting the consulting industry is difficult. Many consulting firms provide other, non-consulting services; many non-consulting businesses provide consulting services. The Management Consultancies Association in the UK dealt with this

Table 1.2 **Forecast growth in the legal services industry, 2008–13**

	2008	2013	% change
Size of the global market ($bn)	581	716	23
Number of lawyers ('000)	2,755	3,033	10
Revenue per lawyer ($'000)	210,779	236,070	12

Sources: Datamonitor; authors' analysis

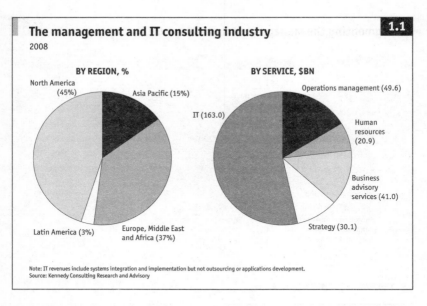

The management and IT consulting industry `1.1`
2008

BY REGION, %

North America (45%)
Asia Pacific (15%)
Latin America (3%)
Europe, Middle East and Africa (37%)

BY SERVICE, $BN

Operations management (49.6)
IT (163.0)
Human resources (20.9)
Business advisory services (41.0)
Strategy (30.1)

Note: IT revenues include systems integration and implementation but not outsourcing or applications development.
Source: Kennedy Consulting Research and Advisory

problem by classifying consulting firms in six groups, acknowledging that today's consulting industry spans a wide array of firms, some of which undertake only management consulting work, but many of which are part of larger firms that offer other services such as systems development, outsourcing, audit, tax, corporate finance and engineering consulting (Figure 1.2 and Table 1.3).

Like the legal services industry, demand for management and IT consulting is expected to grow once the immediate recession is over. But not every type of firm will benefit from this. Type C firms account for around half the industry, although their share has been falling slightly over several years. Their loss has been the gain of Type A firms. Three out of the Big Four firms (Ernst & Young, KPMG and PricewaterhouseCoopers) divested their consulting practices around 2000, but all three have been rebuilding them. Their growth has been higher than the market average as they have started to regain their market share and they now account for around 15% of the market. The fortunes of Type M firms are more varied, as many are smaller specialists. However, including the main strategy firms, this segment still generates around 20% of the market.

The accounting and financial advisory industry
Just as consulting firms do not just do consulting, accounting firms do

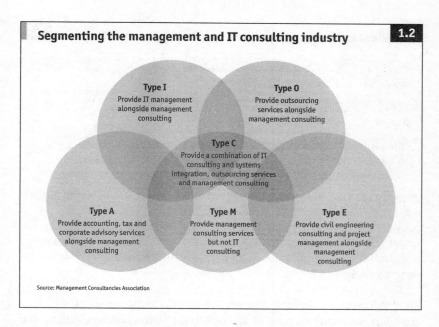

Segmenting the management and IT consulting industry

1.2

Type I
Provide IT management alongside management consulting

Type O
Provide outsourcing services alongside management consulting

Type C
Provide a combination of IT consulting and systems integration, outsourcing services and management consulting

Type A
Provide accounting, tax and corporate advisory services alongside management consulting

Type M
Provide management consulting services but not IT consulting

Type E
Provide civil engineering consulting and project management alongside management consulting

Source: Management Consultancies Association

not just do accounting; they also help organisations develop budgets and prepare tax returns; they may provide corporate finance services and internal audit functions. Revenue in the accounting and financial advisory

Table 1.3 **Examples of consulting firms in each segment**

Type I	Large-scale ERP and other software vendors, such as Oracle and SAP
Type C	Accenture, Capgemini, CSC Computer Sciences Corporation, IBM, Logica
Type O	Capita, Serco, Tribal
Type A	The Big Four firms: Deloitte, Ernst & Young, KPMG and PricewaterhouseCoopers Some mid-sized accountancies, such as Grant Thornton and PKF
Type M	The main strategy firms: Bain, Booz Allen Hamilton, Booz & Co, the Boston Consulting Group and McKinsey & Co Mix-sized strategy firms: OC&C, LEK HR firms: Mercer, Towers Watson, Hay Group Boutique management consultancies
Type E	Arup, Halcrow, Mott MacDonald

Table 1.4 **The Big Four firms, 2008**

	Revenue ($bn)	% change 2008/07
PricewaterhouseCoopers	26.2	−5
Deloitte	26.1	−5
Ernst & Young	21.4	−7
KPMG	20.1	−11

Source: Big4.com

industry is estimated to be around $270 billion in 2008, and recent growth rates have been lower than in consulting and legal services. Datamonitor puts the compound annual growth rate between 2004 and 2008 at just under 5%. It also estimates that traditional audit services accounted for only half of the overall market, and that 54% of revenues come from the Americas and 35% from Europe.

The industry is dominated by the Big Four accounting firms – Deloitte, Ernst & Young, KPMG and PricewaterhouseCoopers – each of which in 2008 had revenues in excess of $20 billion (see Table 1.4). Together, the Big Four firms employ more than 600,000 accountants and other financial advisers. As with the industry as a whole, audits generate half of these firms' income, and this has not changed significantly in recent years.

Regulation makes audit the most stable market, in terms of both the work involved and the fees generated. Although accounting standards vary over time, such adjustments do not affect the underlying aim or form of the audit: "conceptually at least it has not changed much in recent memory" is how one Big Four auditor put it.

Growth has instead come from tax services, often in connection with mergers and acquisitions, and advisory services, as these firms have expanded into risk management and consulting, often in response to regulatory change. The Enron debacle famously exposed the sometimes uncomfortable relationship between these two sets of services. Driven by a genuine business need as much as the desire to grow, some audit firms found themselves in a position with some clients where the independence of their audit might be seen to have been compromised by the level of fees being earned from their non-audit work. In the United States, the Sarbanes-Oxley Act was intended to draw a line in this particular stretch of sand, restricting the level of non-audit fees that could be earned by an organisation's auditor. In practice, this has meant that audit companies focus the sale and delivery of non-audit services to non-audit clients, carefully ring-fencing their interaction where they do hold the audit. However, almost every corporate bankruptcy or financial crisis prompts demands for new regulation, increasing the challenge accounting firms face of balancing regulatory compliance with commercial necessity.

The other source of growth has been emerging economies. For Big Four firms, Asia-Pacific is the fastest growing region. As countries such as India, China and Brazil become bigger markets for such services, the firms in those growing markets need to acquaint themselves with best practice and learn from the experience of those in other countries that have a longer and more extensive history of buying professional services. The alternative is that they learn purely from their own experience how easy it is to waste money on outcomes that disappoint if such services are not procured and managed intelligently.

The distinctive characteristics of professional services

Almost everyone likes to describe themselves as a professional these days and precisely what the terms "profession" and "professional" mean is not clear.

In the strictest sense, a professional is someone who has successfully completed a programme of training and examinations accredited to a professional association. However, this definition covers only careers such as accounting, architecture, engineering, law and medicine, whereas "professional services" is widely used to refer to management consulting, advertising and many other activities. Being a "professional" adds kudos and is a convenient way of justifying higher fees. But it also implies the use of specialist knowledge and work that is, in business, based around projects, which has both tangible and intangible aspects.

Knowledge and customised services

Professional services firms are knowledge-based. The more specialist the advice being sought, the less likely it is that organisations have this skill in-house; and the more specialist the advisers, the more they charge. The expertise they sell changes over time. The Boston Consulting Group, for example, made a lot of money in the 1970s hiring out consultants to build spreadsheets, because the software and skills involved were scarce. As those skills became widely available, the firm had to develop new expertise to sell to its clients, just as any professional services firm has to innovate in order to survive. Law firms which used to gain a significant proportion of their revenue from simple property conveyancing, often done by junior staff, have seen that side of their business eroded by new firms entering the market to provide a standardised service.

Most people would not consider a company that makes computer software, for example, to be a professional services firm, but they would class an IT consultancy as one. This is because IT consultants are not selling a standardised package but are employed to review an organisation's unique set of requirements and suggest ways to improve its systems; their advice will be different for every organisation they work with. The more customised the service, and the more important the technical skills and experience involved, the more likely it is to be perceived as a professional service. The more standardised a service is, and the more it is carried out by relatively junior staff, the less likely it is to be thought so. Furthermore, a professional service is usually expected to possess the capacity to be innovative, though it may not be (or need to be).

Project-based working

External professional advisers have to deliver specific pieces of work or results by specific deadlines. Internal managers have to look to the long term and are likely to have responsibility for several different streams of work. External advisers work for their firm, not their clients, giving them independence but limiting their ability to act: they cannot just tell someone on their client's staff to do something. Internal managers have more authority, but find it harder to step back and take an objective view.

Outside advisers are focused on their project. Unless it is specified otherwise (and often even if it has been), they look at the inputs and outputs of that project in isolation. "If you want to implement a new performance management regime in the next two months, we can do that for you, but it won't leave us time to look at how the changes are communicated to your staff," they may say.

In the past, the project-based nature of much professional services firms' work was at the heart of their clients' complaints; there was a perception that advisers wrote reports or made unrealistic recommendations and did not take on responsibility for their implementation. Conversely, the project-based nature of the work means that professional advisers are more likely to get something done quickly, if only because they are not pulled in a variety of directions as a manager may be. One of the main reasons organisations bring in outside advisers is because they can focus on a particular issue and will not be distracted by other work.

Lack of clarity about the role of an adviser can lead to an adviser being used to perform a long-term, line-management role. This may have short-term advantages: the adviser is immediately available, already knows the lie of the land and will not cost the client a recruitment fee. But the costs of an external adviser's services are likely to be much higher than the remuneration package of an employee. Consultants, for example, offer clients what Christopher McKenna, in *The World's Newest Profession*, calls "economies of knowledge". The experience they amass from previous clients is offered to the next client at a fraction of the cost that client would incur in training an employee. But the advantage of such economies clearly erodes over time: the longer the same professional adviser is on site, the lower is their net value. Of course, professional firms see things differently. One of the biggest operational challenges they face is having people underutilised, so the promise of full-time fees for a year's secondment can be irresistible.

Intangible services

Professional services can be hard to define and their value is difficult to measure. Moreover, their quality will be judged differently by different people: a client who is an expert in a particular field may be less satisfied with a firm's services than one who is a comparative novice. An intangible service is also different from a tangible one in terms of the level of risk involved. Clients that ask an IT company to design, develop and install a new IT system can, quite rightly, put almost all the responsibility for delivering the system onto the supplier. But those that ask the company just to specify a system, so that they can choose and install the appropriate application themselves, cannot expect the IT company to be responsible for the end result. Intangible services require careful thought in terms of who does what and who carries the risk.

For some time professional services firms have been under pressure to make their services more tangible. Clients are frustrated with outside advisers' lack of accountability and are increasingly reluctant to commission them unless they are convinced that there will be a clear return on investment. As a result, professional services firms have sought to differentiate themselves more effectively. In the consulting industry many of the largest consulting firms now offer both advice and implementation. They may help clients develop their outsourcing strategy, but they will also offer to provide the outsourced service; they may review the efficiency of their clients' data centres, but they also have people who can step in to reconfigure them. Some consulting firms have found it hard to isolate the "advisory" element, and they are aware that it would account for only

Classification of professional services 1.3

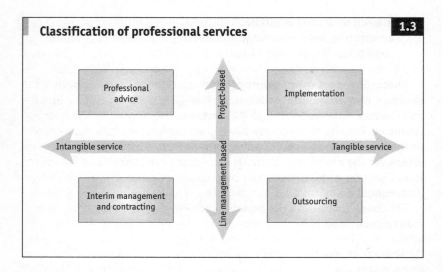

a small proportion of total revenue. The same trend is apparent among legal and audit firms. A law firm will now offer strategic tax planning and compliance work and an audit firm will offer internal audit services. These are activities that clients used to do for themselves and they blur the distinction between intangible advice and tangible implementation.

Despite this trend, there is still a difference between a firm that primarily delivers an intangible service and one whose main function is to execute a particular programme of work such as an advertising campaign.

Classifying professional services

With all this in mind, professional services firms are involved in four main types of work (see Figure 1.3):

◢ Professional advice is customised, intangible and project-based; for the most part, it is advisory (tax, management and IT consulting; accountancy; project management; corporate finance; engineering consulting).

◢ Implementation includes standardised and tangible projects, such as installing computer systems, designing a building that has to conform to specific regulations or running an advertising campaign.

◢ Outsourcing is the delivery of a standardised and tangible service over a long period, often where a third party takes over the running of a specific function.

◪ Interim managers are individuals who plug temporary gaps in an organisational hierarchy, sometimes for a matter of months, sometimes for a couple of years.

There are cross-overs among categories; for example, an interim manager may sometimes work as an associate for a consulting firm or an IT consultancy may need to draw on a contractor when it is short of resources. Equally, people may like to cast themselves in different roles, so interim managers and IT contractors may call themselves consultants whenever the mood suits them. However, people cannot just call themselves lawyers or physicians and practice as "freelances" without formal professional qualifications.

This book focuses on the services provided by law, accountancy, and management and IT consultancy firms, but much of the analysis and advice in it can be applied to other professional services provided by those such as quantity surveyors, architects, engineers, public relations firms, and so on.

2 Why organisations buy professional services

There are three common reasons for buying professional services: specialist skills, intellectual capability and tried-and-tested processes. But sometimes organisations pay good money for services they do not need.

Specialist skills

Knowledge is the bedrock of a professional services firm; it is the first thing clients mention when asked why they brought in external advisers. Such knowledge comes in several forms:

- **Technical know-how.** Some areas of professional advice (tax, accounting, the law) require an understanding of specific rules and regulations, and the advisers involved in them will often have specialist qualifications and take care to keep up to date on changes and developments. Organisations call on this expertise either when they lack it themselves or, perhaps because a particular course of action is high-risk, when they need a second opinion.
- **Solution know-how.** This is similar to technical know-how but is less formalised and therefore harder to evaluate. An example would be a consultant's specialist knowledge of supply chain management: how distribution systems work, inventory management, and so on. A consultant may have a related master's degree or professional diploma, though ultimately there is no single set of rules to learn.
- **Market know-how.** Consultants often need to have or develop a deep understanding of the client's sector as it will immediately suggest a solution to the client's problem or will enable one to be worked towards when it is not clear. There are, of course, common features across sectors, but it is the specific features that must be understood. For example, public-sector organisations are audited differently from those in the private sector; financial institutions have particular processes and technology; clinical trials by pharmaceutical companies are tightly controlled by regulation.

These different types of knowledge are not mutually exclusive. Consulting engineers helping to make sure a shopping mall has a low carbon footprint need their engineering knowledge (technical know-how), an understanding of how to measure a carbon footprint (solution know-how) and the ability to analyse how people shop (market know-how). An accountant needs to be qualified to audit a bank (technical know-how) and also to understand financial instruments (market know-how) and the systems that capture information about them (solution know-how). Such knowledge does, however, come from different sources, and this is significant when purchasing processional services.

Technical know-how is largely an individual matter: individuals study, take an exam and gain a qualification. They may be part of a "qualified" firm, as lawyers and accountants are, but the qualification they have applies to them as a person. Solution know-how depends on colleagues (if clients knew how to solve an issue, they would not need external advisers to help them). It relies on being able to talk to and work with other people who have solved or are trying to solve the same problem elsewhere. Market know-how comes from working with clients.

Intellectual horsepower

Rather than offering standard packages, professional advisers tailor what they do to suit the unique circumstances of their clients. This means that specialist skills, although important, are rarely sufficient. Clients also want their advisers to solve problems, think on their feet, and spot unnoticed threats or opportunities. This capability can take many forms:

◪ **Independence, creative thinking and problem solving.** A client might hire lawyer A (a relatively junior one) to draft a contract but turn to lawyer B (a much more senior one) for advice on a complex deal. Lawyer B has been through the same training as lawyer A and they are both tied to the same body of law, but lawyer B earns higher fees because of the ability to put together a creative solution, be a sharper negotiator and be better able to read human nature. Tax accountant C excels at designing transfer pricing schemes, but a colleague, tax accountant D, is better at answering the objections inevitably raised by the tax authorities. Both are working with the same rules, but tax accountant D can think creatively in a tight corner. Intellectual horsepower is a personal thing. People have it or they do not. It is not something they can acquire at a business school or absorb from colleagues, though both may be instrumental in stimulating an underused intellect.

■ **Facilitation and communication.** The best communicators and facilitators hone their skills by talking to and working with clients. They know how to read the body language of senior managers and cut through pointless board discussions; the best communicators know how to get their message across to frontline staff and middle managers as well as chief executives. Clients hire advisers for these skills, but they might not always admit it. The business case for hiring someone who can talk to your colleagues will always look weak on paper, but it is a hugely important aspect of professional services nonetheless.

■ **Information and analysis.** Individual professional advisers provide "soft" capabilities, but the firms they often work for offer something more tangible: information gathered from third parties or proprietary sources that their clients do not have access to, such as benchmarking data collected from past clients, analysis of recent economic and market trends, and much more. This is the preserve of the big firms; it is not something that a small-town legal firm or freelance consultant can provide.

As with specialist skills, these qualities are not mutually exclusive, but they do stem from different sources: the abilities of individual advisers; breadth of experience in the marketplace; a firm's collective intellectual capital.

Execution and implementation

One of the most significant trends in professional services over the past decade has been the shift from pure advice to implementation. In this context, clients are looking for the following:

■ **Speed.** A professional services firm can marshal a team of people quickly to focus on a specific issue or opportunity. As a result, they can help to accelerate processes: the lawyer's skill can get the acquisition deal done more quickly; the IT consultant can get the new system up and running sooner; the accountant can get a new budgeting process in place in time for the annual planning cycle. None of these people are doing something organisations could not do for themselves with enough time and money; they are just doing it faster.

◪ **Energy and momentum.** A client may look to professional advisers to ensure that a project, once started, is finished. External advisers can dedicate themselves to the project, whereas the client's employees usually have other responsibilities to distract them.

◪ **A road map.** Organisations may know what they want to do but not how to do it, in which case they look to professional advisers to provide a plan they can follow to help them implement a new idea, avoid the pitfalls of past failures, or follow "best practice".

These different needs demand different skills and resources, which come from the individual adviser (speed), from the breadth of experience in the market (energy and momentum) and the firm itself (road map). Table 2.1 summarises the three main reasons organisations buy professional services. It is clear that some of the attributes required relate to the individual adviser, some to the firm and some to the individual or firm's market experience. These distinctions are important in avoiding the risk of misusing professional advisers.

Table 2.1 **Summary of client needs**

Client need	Individual's characteristics	Market experience	Firm's intellectual assets
Specialist skills	Technical know-how	Market know-how	Solution know-how
Intellectual horsepower	Independence, creative thinking and problem solving	Facilitation and communication	Information and analysis
Execution and implementation	Speed	Energy and momentum	A road map

The misuse of professional services firms

There are occasions when professional services firms are engaged inappropriately, when the outcome is unlikely to represent good value for money. Reasons this happens include:

◪ **The need for a potential scapegoat.** When an organisation needs to do something difficult or where the likelihood of failure is high, engaging professional services support – often management consultants – provides a manager with cover in case the result is not successful. When it is not, the manager can then resort to the classic excuse: "Well, the consultants said we should do it."

◪ **Decision to be rubber-stamped.** This is typical in cases where the outcome is likely to be positive. An organisation may lack confidence in its own abilities or not trust the judgment of its own staff and therefore gets consultants to, in effect, make the decision. However, getting expert legal advice may be sensible risk management and using outsiders to help clear a log-jam in internal decision-making can be vital. This makes it hard to determine where good management stops and rubber-stamping starts.

◪ **Delaying tactics.** Professional services firms can be brought in as a means of prevarication. A head office may insist on an organisational change, but a local managing director, unhappy about the plans, suggests that they should be reviewed by external advisers in the hope that this will postpone the process, perhaps until the sponsor of the change has moved on to other matters.

However, the single biggest cause of professional service firms being misused is egotism. Some managers clearly relish having intelligent and expensive consultants at their beck and call and may perceive that arriving at a meeting with "their" strategy partner in tow gains them prestige among their peers. By contrast, many senior people simply value having a trusted adviser whom they can use as a sounding board.

All this matters because it is easy, especially during the purchase process, for clients to confuse their underlying need (specialist skill, intellectual horsepower or execution and implementation) with the skills required to deliver it (individual, market or firm-related). If an organisation needs access to a specialist skill, what kind of skill is it looking for: technical know-how, market know-how or solutions know-how – or a combination of these? Is it evaluating the firm or the adviser? If it is looking for specialist skills, what use is the thick volume of client references unless they apply to the individual being considered? If it is looking for market know-how, how can it be sure that the person it might be hiring can tap into the firm's reservoir of expertise?

The irony is that the services where the technical skills of the individual matter most and are most easily evaluated (law, accountancy) are also those that, primarily for reasons of regulation, clients tend to buy from a firm rather than from a freelance adviser. By contrast, those services where the collective experience of the firm is as important as that of the individual (some types of consulting) are also those where clients can choose to hire individuals (freelance consultants).

The implications for buying: demand management

One important function of purchasing is to ensure that it is carried out as efficiently and cost-effectively as possible. In most cases, this is reactive: the buying team is told what and approximately how much is needed, and it is that team's job to liaise with suppliers and ensure value for money. When buying teams are instructed to cut costs, they consolidate suppliers, negotiate discounts and so on. What they do not generally do is question the demand: it is for the organisation to say how much it needs and for purchasing to obtain it. If the need to reduce costs is greater than the amount likely to be saved by cutting prices, responsibility falls on the organisation to find a way to reduce demand. In other words, if an organisation needs to reduce the amount of money it spends on office supplies by a small amount, it can ask its buying team to get a bigger discount; but if it wants to reduce its expenditure significantly, it has to change the way it works.

This is also true where professional services are concerned. However, organisations frequently struggle to reduce their demand for professional advice, except where there is a clear and unequivocal ban on its use at the most senior level. There are several reasons for this, some reasonable, some less so:

- **Part of the solution, not part of the problem.** For an organisation that is trying to cut costs, the amount of money spent on IT or office supplies will always be part of the problem. They are expenses that need to be minimised; the less the organisation can spend on them, while still doing the things it needs to do, the better. Professional services are different because expenditure on them may help save money, either because the organisation does not have to hire a full-time member of staff or retrain an existing employee, or because their advice might cut costs or increase revenues.
- **Reliance.** Although professional advisers are mostly supposed to offer specialist skills and input for a short time, many organisations come to rely on them for longer. Decades of cost-cutting and periodic recruitment freezes mean that managers rarely have spare capacity at their disposal, so using outside help, even for considerable periods, may be the only solution.

◘ **Invisibility.** For a long time, expenditure on professional services was recorded neither separately nor consistently, or was coded as "other" expenditure or labelled temporary labour. It was therefore hard for people to cut what they could not see. Today organisations are more likely to want to scrutinise their spending on professional services and insist it is coded properly, but some still struggle to track it in any helpful way.

◘ **Discretionary expenditure.** The discretionary nature of many professional services makes them, ironically, harder to cut. Everyone has to agree that they do not need a particular service before it can be dispensed with and to measure the value of most professional services. A chief information officer (CIO) who has hired a consulting firm to review the department's costs may see such expenditure as necessary, but the HR director may not. Even if the HR director wins the immediate argument, the CIO may return to it some months later or "re-scope" the work so that it still gets done.

◘ **Status.** The CIO may want the IT consultants there because there is work to do, but his motivation may be just as much that having them around makes him feel more important in a way that spending more on office supplies or even IT equipment does not.

Purchasing departments therefore have a particularly important role to play in the case of professional services, but it is quite different from that which they perform in many other areas. Instead of coming in at a point when the organisation has decided what it wants, the department has to be involved in an intelligent discussion about what is needed and the nature of the resources required to meet that need.

What is needed?

When an organisation discusses what it needs from its advisers, the focus should be on what value they can add that the organisation cannot sensibly add itself, given the starting premise that an organisation can do anything it wants by itself, given sufficient time, effort and investment. Once the underlying rationale for using external help is clear, it is easier to identify what resources are most appropriate.

As Figure 2.1 illustrates, an organisation may require the input of a firm or an individual, or a combination of the two. If it is looking for information and analysis, it may need the knowledge base of a firm but not necessarily an experienced person carrying out the analysis; a bright young

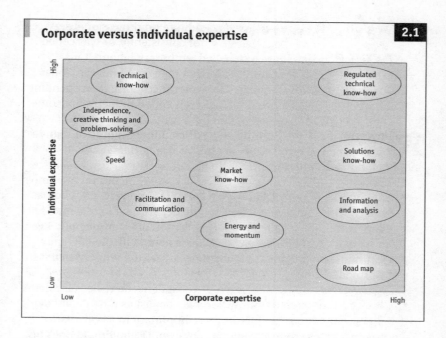

Corporate versus individual expertise **2.1**

- High — Individual expertise — Low
- Low — Corporate expertise — High

Technical know-how

Regulated technical know-how

Independence, creative thinking and problem-solving

Speed

Solutions know-how

Market know-how

Facilitation and communication

Information and analysis

Energy and momentum

Road map

statistician may be just as good. If it wants objective, technical advice on a specific issue, it may be able to get this from a suitably experienced individual, not necessarily from a big firm. Vast sums of clients' money are wasted by getting experienced individuals to do work that could be done just as well by junior staff according to an appropriate method or procedure. Similarly, money is wasted by paying premium rates to a firm when what is really needed is an experienced freelancer.

3 The challenges of buying professional services

Buying services is different not only from buying products but also from buying any other kinds of service. To do it well, the following should be borne in mind:

- The services provided can have a major impact on the success or failure of the purchasing organisation.
- The services are usually provided to senior, smart, well-paid individuals by other senior, smart, well-paid individuals.
- Only some professional services are regulated in what has to be provided; most are tailored to meet the needs of individual organisations.
- Lack of information about such things as a firm's track record in a particular field or the fees it typically charges for similar work makes it hard to compare and evaluate professional services firms.
- The outcome of using external advisers depends as much on the end-user as the adviser and, to a large extent, on the relationship between the two.

Leverage

Buying a stapler involves no risk: at worst, if it does not work it can be replaced, perhaps by one of a different make. The risk exposure with a cleaning contract is much the same: it will be obvious if the office is not cleaned properly, in which case the answer is to complain or change supplier. Should an employee slip on a wet floor and break a leg because a cleaner forgot to leave out a warning sign, the liability should be covered by insurance. But if a law firm advising on an acquisition misses a mistake in a crucial clause and the oversight is exploited by a competitor, scuppering the deal, the damage and opportunity cost may be huge, far outweighing the legal fees involved. Even if it can be demonstrated that the firm has been negligent, it is unlikely that any damages paid will take into account the opportunity cost.

One of the features of professional services is that there can be a vast difference between the fees charged and the value created or destroyed. A professional firm will try to limit its liability, typically to the fees charged or an agreed multiple of them, whereas a client is equally likely to want to expose the firm to unlimited liability.

Top-level involvement

The potential for professional services work to create or destroy value means that it is overseen by people at an appropriately senior level in the client organisation, often board directors or the people who report directly to them.

But status plays a role as well. Some professional services are rather like luxury items that, in the past, would have been available to only a small number of wealthy people. Over time, however, access to them has widened, with aspiring middle managers now bringing "their" advisers in. Hiring a "magic circle" law firm or a strategic consultancy is still a badge of, if not quite honour, then certainly achievement. Clearly, professional services firms are not averse to such associations: much of their marketing is designed to send a subliminal message that the people who buy their services are the cognoscenti, members of an exclusive club in which smart people work with other smart people. Those in a purchasing department do not have automatic right of entry into this "club".

Regulation, or the lack of it

Some professional services are governed by regulation; for example, on the requirement and form of company audits, which must be supervised by someone who has a recognised qualification. But many are not, such as much of the work done by management or IT consultants (see Table 3.1). Those who work in the professions are of course required to follow the law but they are often self-regulated, as is the case with the legal profession, which in most countries controls the examination system that leads to a professional qualification. For those involved in such activities as management or IT consultancy there are no qualifications they must have or professional bodies to which they must belong, but some firms try to compensate for this by developing their own training programmes. For example, a software company may accredit consultants in its implementation process and a strategic consultancy may have a standard process for carrying out due diligence in mergers and acquisitions. The more a firm would like to position its services as must-haves, rather than nice-to-haves, the more likely it is to have developed some type of quasi regulation of its own.

Regulated services are easier to buy than unregulated ones in that

Table 3.1 **Regulating professional services**

	External regulation	Internal regulation	No regulation
Need	Essential to the well-being of an individual, corporation or society	Essential if objectives are to be achieved	Desirable if objectives are to be achieved
Choice	None, use of services is essential and/or legally mandatory	Discretionary, but high risk not to use	Discretionary
Regulatory body	Government-driven, external and independent	Professional body; self-regulating	None
Accreditation	Mandatory, overseen by regulatory body	Mandatory, overseen by regulatory body	None, except that provided by firms themselves
Examples	Medicine Statutory audits	Law Chartered surveyors	IT services Management consulting

regulation creates standardisation. Unregulated services are usually non-standard, making it harder to compare suppliers and evaluate proposals. But this is not a reason for greater regulation.

Audits are easier to buy than advice on corporate finance. Because they are standardised, comparing the technical skills of audit teams is comparatively straightforward. The skills of corporate financiers are much harder to assess. Standardising them might make it simpler for purchasers, but it would result in an inferior service because corporate finance teams would be required to follow the same procedure, irrespective of the circumstances and needs of their clients – and one size will not fit all.

Eric Abrahamson is an American academic who has studied the impact of management fads on the organisations that adopt them. Looking at many companies over a long period, he concluded that the early adopters of such fads benefited more than later adopters. The main reason for the differences was that early adopters took more care in deciding whether a new management tool was relevant to their business and were much more likely to customise it to fit their specific needs. The value of the tool lay in the extent to which it could be adapted to the business, that it was not standardised. Trying to standardise the tool would destroy much of its

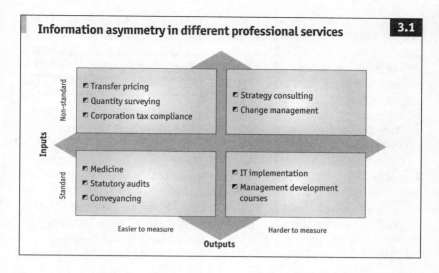

Information asymmetry in different professional services   3.1

Inputs

Non-standard
- Transfer pricing
- Quantity surveying
- Corporation tax compliance

- Strategy consulting
- Change management

Standard
- Medicine
- Statutory audits
- Conveyancing

- IT implementation
- Management development courses

Easier to measure   Harder to measure

Outputs

value. Moreover, the quality of service received will be influenced by the commissioning approach. Negotiate a consulting firm down too hard on rates and you will not get their best people on your projects.

Asymmetric information

Because most professional services are intangible with hard-to-define benefits, organisations find it hard to judge the quality of the services they are considering before they buy them. The situation is complicated by several factors. Clients may not have access to enough information on the skills and experience of the individuals they are about to hire. Consulting firms are likely only to have forwarded positive references from previous clients, quietly ignoring occasions on which they have been less successful. Even where full disclosure is promised, short of carrying out a full-scale due diligence process, a client has little means of verifying what it has been told. Client confidentiality, sometimes justified, but equally often driven by an unwillingness to admit to problems, makes it hard for both sides to learn from past experience. In the absence of more reliable and objective data, clients rely on the overall reputation of a firm or the recommendation of a colleague.

The extent of the problem varies with the type of service provided. As Figure 3.1 illustrates, lack of information for the buyers of a given service may relate to a service's inputs or outputs or both.

Where a service involves following a standard set of instructions or working in an environment which is constant for all organisations (the law, for instance), a high level of information will be available to all those involved. By contrast, where the inputs are different in each project, it is much harder to specify in advance exactly how the project as a whole will work. The advisers may be able to draw on their past experience and various tools and techniques, but the pieces of the puzzle will never come together in the same shape twice. Non-standard inputs make it difficult for buyers and suppliers to specify and agree the nature and scope of the services to be provided.

For work that has measurable outputs, it is possible to put together a business case which calculates the likely return on investment. Lack of measurable outputs makes it hard for people who buy professional services to create a business case, compare consulting firms and make sure that they are paying a reasonable price. It makes it difficult, too, for organisations to improve the way they buy and use professional services because there is no reliable standard against which to evaluate their performance.

Quality of delivery depends on relationships

"We're a relationship business," say professional services firms. Look at any of their websites and you will see the same set of qualities highlighted: the technical excellence of their people; their openness, integrity and professionalism; the extent to which they can think laterally, creatively and globally. They can also, as if all this was not enough, work with your own staff so seamlessly and effectively that you will find it hard to see where one team starts and the other finishes.

But relationships push up prices because buyers are reluctant to negotiate with people they like; they obscure business cases because it is harder to get rid of people who are already working with you; they reduce competition because you end up buying from the same suppliers again and again. Relationships complicate the purchasing process because they make it harder to be objective. While you can use a semi-scientific process for evaluating proposals and presentations, these do not take gut feel into account. Indeed, in many cases, they become a means by which gut instinct can be justified rather than a way to challenge it.

It is also the case, to some extent at least, that the delivery of high-quality professional services depends on relationships. A lawyer who does not get on with a client may be less willing to take the latter's late-night phone call. A tax adviser who enjoys working with a particular finance director will be more likely to put in the extra effort that success often requires. A consulting firm that knows its way around a client's organisation is better positioned than a rival that has never worked there before to know how to negotiate the internal politics. Purchasing managers therefore find themselves caught between a rock and a hard place. On the one hand, they need to maintain a professional distance during the purchasing process, but on the other, they need to make sure that there is an effective working relationship between client and adviser.

Buying consulting in the financial services sector

Cameron Smith has had ten years of senior experience buying professional services in the financial services sector. He now runs his own consulting practice, LLPS Consulting.

Before the credit crunch struck, banks were some of the world's largest buyers of professional services in the world, particularly consulting. Smith says:

I used to work at Ford. In that kind of organisation, purchasing is key because if the right parts don't arrive when they are needed you can't make new cars: the supply chain is incredibly important. When people moved from buying car parts to buying marketing, human resources and professional services, they'd try to use the same approach, breaking things down into their components. But in professional services you're often buying a whole that's greater than the sum of the parts. In marketing, you might be looking for the kind of people who can design and run a vibrant high-energy campaign. In IT, you might not only need strong technical and implementation capability, but also a huge cross-section of skills which can be called on when required: you're buying depth of experience.

In these circumstances, Smith knows, you have to adopt a different approach:

How can you tell if someone really knows what they're talking about? It's hard to measure and you have to rely on an element of gut feel. The key is information, the more you give them about what you want and get from them in terms of what they've done, the better the decision you're likely to make.

But Smith also recognises that other, less rational factors come into play:

If a provider's done great work and built strong relationships with the people he's worked with, almost to the point of dependency, and you arrive on the scene, then he's probably going to try and bypass you and go directly to his friend at the top and you'll find yourself doing nothing more than filling in purchase orders day after day. That means you need personal credibility with the people at the top: you have to work with them, rather than tell them what to do. If they're dead set on a particular firm, then you get them to explain why and suggest alternative options. Understanding the supplier market is critical, as is the recognition that you can't win every battle but that, the more you are perceived to be making credible challenges to them, not just being an obstacle, the more likely they are to start taking your advice.

In Smith's experience, the first step should always be to find out how much the organisation actually spends on external advice around the world and what the money was spent on. "It is essentially a mopping-up exercise," he says. "Most organisations don't have a precise and reliable figure for this." Misclassified expenditure makes the job hard: the process typically takes months "because people don't know how to code this expenditure". But organisational complexity makes it even harder. In most banks, procurement is a central support function with no profit and loss responsibility. Without any central remit, it has to tap into the budgets of each business unit and aggregate the results. The best it can do is report information.

The situation is completely different where the purchasing team become part of a profit centre: what they do then has a direct impact on performance. He recalls the impact of this change in one organisation:

The first thing the chief executive asked us to do was to put together a pack of information on our top 100 suppliers in terms of volume of business: what our expenditure was, what kind of contracts we had, what we could do to contain or reduce expenditure. There were six pages to every supplier, which gives you an idea of how serious a piece of analysis this was. From it, we were able to form a view of which areas were under control and which weren't. It also provided us with the evidence to start to change the culture of the organisation and to influence people's behaviour. We'd had all the processes in place before but people would find ways round them; what we got then was our chief executive saying unequivocally that all consulting would stop unless it was something we had to do for regulatory reasons. The chief executive sent an email saying that every consulting project, however small, had to be justified either directly to him or to the CFO: it was the corporate equivalent of walking quietly, but carrying a big stick.

To make such a ban enforceable required the support of senior management and a clear definition of what was, and what was not, consulting.

We recognised that people might need short-term help, but we wanted to ensure that where they were essentially body-shopping, we weren't incurring the expense of the intellectual capital, marketing and branding of a big-name professional firm. The problem was that there hadn't been a clear definition.

These days, the company is clear that consulting means independent, third-party advice by suppliers who come to solve problems and to provide independent advice around specific issues. Smith says:

Body-shopping refers to people who come and work at our direction, behest and control for a fixed period. The language you use makes a huge difference: if you shift from saying that the work is theirs to saying they're supporting ours, then you've moved from consulting to staff augmentation and transferred risk and responsibility to us, to boot.

Getting everyone to abide by this definition meant working with suppliers as well as internal managers.

The focus then moved to complete compliance with the procurement rules on all sides:

If we found someone had brought a firm without going through the proper process we could take that straight to the chief executive – and we did. The difference between what the organisation now spends and what it used to spend is quite incredible: there are virtually no contractors left and the overall level of expenditure on professional services has come down dramatically – which we can, of course, now measure because we went through that base-lining exercise two years ago.

The result has been a change in culture:

People no longer assume that if you want to get something done, you bring in a consultant. Instead of assuming that we have to do everything, we prioritise: people do get swamped with work, but the key is to work out what's important and get rid of the things that aren't, rather than to bring in extra resources.

If anything, it is the culture of the supply side that has proved harder to change. Smith says:

I worked as a solicitor for a while, and the partner I worked for used to visit his clients in his expensive BMW. To me, that sends the wrong message because your clients think they've paid for it and they resent it. The professional firms we deal with have lovely, expensive offices and they'll tell us they need them if they're to attract the best people, but such ostentatious expenditure doesn't sit well, especially in today's market. We have to reduce our costs and we need our suppliers to understand that and work with us.

Professional firms have reacted to this in various ways. Some of the biggest firms have refused to reduce their rates at all, arguing that the value they add is way above the cost of their services. Others have been prepared to offer substantial discounts but only if they are acknowledged as a long-term supplier of choice.

What we're really looking for, and only a minority of firms get this, is for professional firms to cut their cloth according to the times, just as we're doing ourselves. We'd like much greater transparency about what firms provide and how much they charge, but many still feel that even this is beneath them.

Perhaps it is as a result of this disenchantment with some of the larger firms that Smith would like to see further cultural changes on the supply side in the future:

We should be introducing more multi-sourcing, using the bigger firms to bring in the specialist services and skills they don't have from other sources. We tried it before with mixed results, perhaps because we were working with the wrong suppliers who found the idea of going outside their core business an anathema. So it will undoubtedly be a challenge, but if we want to ensure we have access to the best skills at a good rate, this has to be the way forward.

4 The supplier perspective

This book focuses mainly on the purchase of professional services from the buyer's perspective, but the best purchasing managers are those capable of looking at obstacles and opportunities from different angles. They put themselves in others' shoes. This chapter presents the views of a variety of senior people working in different professional firms about the changes they have seen in the purchasing process in recent years.

If the process is too one-sided, neither side will win. Professional firms that have a strong client relationship may charge too much for their services and become complacent. Purchasing managers who pride themselves on getting rock-bottom prices may end up getting rock-bottom quality. If they are to step between their internal customers and professional advisers and still add value, purchasing people have to recognise, if not match, their customers' expertise.

The importance of judgment

The rise of the purchasing function has been highly visible to Stuart Diack, an associate partner in the audit practice at professional services firm Deloitte:

> It's ironic. After all, it is consultants from firms such as Deloitte who have been advising people to streamline their procurement functions, change their terms and conditions, know who their key suppliers are.

Audit is different from most other professional services, not only because it is so heavily regulated but also because the risks involved in making a mistake are so large. "Very few industries have the zero tolerance for failure that there is in the audit business," says Diack. This drives transparency to a level that is comparatively unusual in professional services:

> We have to be clear about quality and risk management. The regulator can look at our audit files and report to our clients and more publicly on the quality of our work.

That changes the role of purchasing:

If you're buying a component for a truck, the way you test its quality is to install it and see how the engine runs. You look at the engine, not the component. The same is true when you're buying an audit: you could spend time looking at the methodology, the people we've got and so on, the equivalent of the component, but the real test is whether the engine runs, and that's what the regulator looks at. You don't have to do the equivalent of a factory visit and, overall, less procurement time is needed.

Another difference is in who the customer for the audit is:

Audits are done for external shareholders, not executive management. My duty as an auditor is not to make the chief executive happy but to report to the shareholders. In practice that means that the choice of audit firm is decided by an audit committee, not the board of directors, so the role for in-house purchasing people is limited.

Although financial audits have been less affected by this change, purchasing people do make their presence felt when it comes to the advisory, but less regulated, services that Deloitte provides. The challenge, Diack believes, is that, where purchasing people are involved, they are not experts:

Purchasing people are typically either professional buyers or negotiators, or lawyers; they're not providers of accounting advice. You can find yourself in situations where you're negotiating with purchasing managers who know less about what's needed and which firms offer that service than their internal customers.

This creates an additional layer of complexity, because end-users and purchasing people may have different views and firms such as Deloitte can end up being caught between the two.

Sometimes it reaches the point where no one is clear – us, the purchasing team or the end-clients – about who has the deciding vote in selecting a firm. That makes the process more protracted, expensive and frustrating for all involved.

Lack of expertise also means that the way in which purchasing managers evaluate firms may be simplistic: without market knowledge and judgment honed by experience to rely on, they can rely too heavily on a process. Indeed, the two are in inverse relationship: the more purchasing managers know, the less they have to rely on process. Diack says:

> But where it's a new or unfamiliar field, human nature will drive people to go by the book. We're very happy to demonstrate our credentials, provide evidence of our processes and so on, but decisions about the best fit between a professional firm and a client will always come down to judgment, and you don't get that in a process.

The involvement of procurement managers

The steel and glass of Slaughter and May's offices belie the fact that the firm was founded 120 years ago. Christopher Saul, the firm's senior partner, says:

> We are a traditional firm with a strongly collegiate culture – but a modern outlook. Every partner is chosen in election meetings attended by all the partners and, after election, is centrally involved in developing his or her own practice without undue direction by management. We are a lockstep firm [in which financial reward is based on the number of years a partner has been at the firm, giving the best rewards to partners with the longest service] and so it is professional pride and peer group pressure, rather than differential rewards, which maintain and drive standards and profits.

The firm's international strategy is also unusual. Rather than opening its own offices in a host of different countries, it has developed deep friendships with leading independent firms outside the UK that share its culture and values.

The increased involvement over recent years of procurement managers within clients has meant that the firm has a new constituency to deal with who are not business executives or lawyers. Saul says:

> We are a service business and highly responsive to clients, so we have no problem in adapting the way we pitch for business to take account of the emergence of procurement teams. For

some clients, however, this has worked better than for others. Sometimes you can see that procurement teams are operating independently of internal business executives and lawyers and this, in turn, can lead to frustration for those executives and lawyers.

Necessarily, procurement teams tend to focus on cost and, specifically, on hourly rates:

We understand, of course, that clients will be under internal and external pressure to watch costs spent with external consultants. However, clients are increasingly sceptical about hourly billing and worry that it can be an incentive to inefficiency and also not necessarily be an appropriate measure of "value" delivered to the business.

Accordingly, finance directors and general counsel are more and more interested in alternative billing techniques which focus more on the value received by the business than the time spent by the service provider.

This means, in Saul's view, that procurement teams will need to focus on working hand-in-hand with the principal executives and lawyers within businesses. This will enable procurement teams to get a keener handle on the different kinds of service provided by different law firms. Firms like Slaughter and May, which seek to develop "multi-specialist lawyers", will be able to field leaner teams and potentially produce a more textured service for the client while expending materially fewer hours. On this basis, the ultimate cost may turn out to be less even if the nominal hourly rates are higher. Saul says:

There is no complacency in any of this as we know that we live in a fiercely competitive world, but close internal co-operation enabling procurement teams to work with different law firm models will aid the overall procurement process.

Changes in purchasing practice

Historically, many of the larger consulting firms have based themselves in Chicago or New York, but North Highland is different. Based in Atlanta, Georgia, it is big enough to be an international firm, but instead it prides itself on being based close to where its clients are, in 19 offices across the United States. Although it is part of a network of firms in other countries which it either owns or partly owns, how have changes in purchasing, often initiated by global clients, affected its business?

Jeff Busch, an executive vice-president at the North Highland company, says:

> Many companies are moving towards approved vendor lists, partly as a means to reduce the fee rates they pay. We understand that, especially in a difficult economic climate. A much greater challenge for us is when they also say that they're only prepared to do business with three or four consulting firms. That's frustrating, because these firms, however big they are, can't service every need or provide the best service. Because these clients only want to work with a small number of firms, the firms they select have to be very large and global. Yet, ironically, most consulting work outside of IT development is still bought and done at a local level.

Busch sees that the ultimate clients, the end-users, are just as frustrated by this trend:

> It's an approach that's come out of IT expenditure and now all professional services are being treated in the same way, despite the fact that services provided by firms like North Highland are much more heterogeneous. Moreover, although end-users understand that purchasing departments are trying to inject greater objectivity into the process, they don't think the latter appreciate that good relationships play an important role in professional services. As a consultant, I have a good personal relationship with my clients and that means that I won't under any circumstances let them down. Also, if we know someone well, we can work with them to help clarify their requirements before they put their RFP [request for proposal] together: some of the best consulting we do is before we sign the contract. Strong relationships aren't always a bad thing.

Despite this, Busch is sanguine about future trends:

> That tension between purchasing people and their internal customers will have to resolve itself in some way. A third and more sophisticated way will emerge in which both sides will

work together and, as part of this, will expect their suppliers to collaborate with them. That's something we see a lot more of in research and development in, for example, the electronics sector. We don't yet see it in consulting.

Problems with procurement people

Jeremy Anderson, head of markets, Europe, at professional services and auditing firm KPMG, cannot forget the first discussion he ever had, as an advisory partner, with a head of procurement:

> It was in a major bank. He said that, if we'd introduce him to our clients – his internal customers [in the bank] – then he'd help us get on the tender list.

Things have moved on since then:

> Procurement people are now a part of life. At best, they're well-informed about our industry and try to build a win-win deal between purchaser and supplier. They focus on getting good value for money and can help us by providing honest feedback about how we've performed in a particular tender or advise us not to waste time bidding for a particular piece of work. They've become a stakeholder group in their own right, and one we have to deal with.

All this depends on procurement teams having a mature understanding of what they are buying:

> Professional services are intangible and it is therefore almost impossible to make an informed decision on the basis of a piece of paper or a proposal, but comes down to the trust between buyers and suppliers. Will we deliver the people, content and enthusiasm required to do the work properly? Can we work with the organisation in a way that creates sustainable value? Can we manage the wider stakeholder group?

Not everyone has the expertise and confidence to do this: some procurement teams can; others recognise their limitations and concentrate on managing the process, leaving the evaluation and decision to the ultimate client. The problem, as Anderson sees it, lies with the procurement teams who fall between these two stools:

They try to contribute to the decision-making process but can only focus on the more mechanistic elements such as price. They also put themselves between us and the end-user, making it harder for us to understand what the latter is really looking for. If you can't get an informed view on the scope of a project, you can end up wasting a lot of time negotiating a piece of work that doesn't fit the requirements. It's much better to talk these things through, discuss what's possible and affordable and come up with a project with which both sides, the client and us, feel comfortable. We need to understand when they're looking for a cheap-and-cheerful solution to a problem they just want to get off the table, and when they're facing an issue of strategic importance. With procurement acting as middle-men, you get misunderstandings – and those cost money.

Anderson's other frustration is with the level of management information professional firms such as KPMG are now required to provide clients, another trend that has been initiated by procurement teams anxious to maintain supervision of projects with which they are not directly involved:

We have to analyse huge amounts of information then present it in a format they require, not one we'd use. How many hours have been worked and by whom? What rates were they billed at? We have to put together different packs for different organisations, much of which has to be done manually.

He suspects this is just information for information's sake, but a bigger worry is that it deflects attention away from whether a professional firm is delivering value: "Cost is only one side of the equation."

Raising the game

"The involvement of purchasing people in buying professional services isn't new," says Mark Leiter, president of professional services and an expert in professional services strategy at The Nielsen Company, a global information and media company. From Leiter's point of view, the involvement of a client's procurement organisation is limited to bigger projects, typically $500,000 or more. But as the amount of money organisations spend on professional services has grown in recent times, so has the proportion of that work coming under the scrutiny of professional buyers. Leiter says:

Another factor has been the changing definition of professional services. A billion-dollar IT outsourcing or systems development contract is clearly a hugely important commercial deal that requires significant scrutiny, but is it a "professional service"? With a professional service, the client relationship is at the core of what you're paying for, but many suppliers now combine such services with ones that include information technology. What's new is the emergence of a new cadre of more informed and sophisticated clients who understand your economics and can coach their own procurement organisations to find key leverage points in any negotiation.

In Leiter's view, this will force professional firms to raise their game and change the way they manage their business:

You have to be able to manage demand, so that when someone asks you for a discount you can look them in the eye and say you're already fully utilised. In the past, firms have fallen over themselves to ensure they have every possible skill available only to find themselves struggling to maintain utilisation. Keeping supply and demand in sync is an essential lesson we've taken away from our procurement experiences.

But in other areas, it is end-users who are driving the changes:

There's more unbundling, with clients drawing a clearer distinction between the things they can do themselves and those where they need external help. Ultimately, this is very smart for our clients while allowing us to focus on doing the work that is in our sweet spot. One of the biggest questions for professional firms dealing with purchasing teams is, do you hold your line on pricing and, if you decide to negotiate, how much information are you prepared to share? Some purchasing departments are requesting an almost insane level of transparency: they want to know how we remunerate our staff, including compensation and benefits. A smart firm knows when to draw the line because it's an unending process and one that forces you to be defensive about trivial details. Some firms get worried that they'll lose the business if they don't agree to this, but each time they share such information they're eroding their negotiating position. Greater transparency doesn't always mean they'll win more business because, ironically, the decision isn't just about price. In this environment – and I can't see any circumstances in which the role of purchasing will decline – you need a distinctive value proposition, one that differentiates you. The clear message you need to send is that, "what you get from me, you can only get from me".

The importance of good relationships

"Relationships work in the client's favour," says David Cheyne, a senior partner at Linklaters, a leading law firm. Clients who know their way around the multi-layered legal industry know which firm to use in which circumstances:

You don't want to use a big firm to do a small deal any more than you want a small firm to work on a big deal. Equally, why co-ordinate the input of a variety of small, local firms when it's simpler to work with one firm that operates globally?

In Cheyne's view, such relationships, based on shared expertise, play a fundamental role in ensuring that clients get the best commercial deal. They are not, as purchasing people often assume, cosy situations in which firms are hired simply because they know the right people:

Clients instruct individuals, not firms, and they don't give work to people they don't like working with. But, however much a client likes us, they're not going to give us the work if they don't think we're the right firm to do it. Having a sophisticated client is not a disadvantage.

A good relationship does not, therefore, guarantee a firm work:

Clients will have more than one relationship. Because their needs vary, it's unlikely that they'd be able to get every service from a single firm. We may work with a particular client on one transaction, then win nothing for a while. Although many organisations have a list of "preferred" law firms, most start from the project in hand and pick the firm that matches their requirements, irrespective of whether they are on the list or not.

Although Linklaters does come across procurement managers who are well-informed. Cheyne says:

> *What we're not sure about is whether the average purchasing manager understands the different services firms provide and what differentiates one law firm from another. Some have come from buying bulk services or products where you can specify your requirements precisely and negotiate a discount without compromising quality. The concept of value for money in a professional services context is more complex: you can end up paying over the odds for routine work and getting poorer quality advice on important transactions.*

Where they lack expertise, procurement managers tend to focus on price, to the detriment of all:

> *There isn't a client in their right mind who doesn't want to know how much they're spending on a given service and whether they get value for it. Greater scrutiny is entirely sensible and right, and we respond to it. But discounts can cut into the quality of service but arrangements where fees are totally dependent on results are potentially even more dangerous. A client has to be confident that their lawyer is giving them the right advice: if the firm has been incentivised to complete a deal, for example, their advice may become biased.*

A better approach would be an informed and frank discussion:

> *Sometimes we can reach the stage where we can say, "Look, it isn't economically sensible for us to do this piece of work and we'll end up being too expensive." It's not good for us, any more than it is for the client, to take on work where the client feels they're paying too much and we feel undervalued.*

PART 2
ROLE OF THE PURCHASING DEPARTMENT

One of the difficulties purchasing teams often face is their relationship with the rest of the organisation. Are they a central support function or should individual buyers sit alongside the people they work with? Are they providing help when asked or are they supposed to intervene in every buying decision? Is their role to provide strategic advice or to deal with contract administration?

When buying professional services, such questions are especially pertinent because of the potentially large impact those services can have on an organisation. It is therefore crucial that:

- purchasing strategy is aligned with overall corporate strategy;
- the service being bought is clearly specified, a process that involves end-users at least as much as buyers;
- buyers act as "business partners", facilitating the process but not allowing important decisions to be taken without due thought or challenge.

5 Aligning the purchasing approach with the business strategy, structure and culture

The development of an effective purchasing approach depends on understanding an organisation's reasons for using professional services firms. But the purchasing approach is unlikely to succeed unless it is aligned with the overarching strategy, culture and structure of the organisation because it will lack credibility not only internally but probably with suppliers too.

For instance, if an organisation, for the moment at least, is concentrating all its efforts on longer-term growth rather than profitability, driving down purchasing costs through tough negotiation with suppliers or aggressive internal demand management will lack resonance with senior management, who are more likely to be interested in how purchasing activities can contribute to growth and new market opportunities. The purchasing department should instead look at what they can do to drive revenue and growth through the mechanisms at their disposal. Which suppliers can bring innovation? Are there opportunities for partnerships with important suppliers? Which professional services firms can help to open up new markets or product areas? Conversely, an organisation in the grip of severe financial uncertainty will see survival as the top priority and purchasing will be expected to help cut costs accordingly.

Kristine Moore, global head of indirect purchasing at Shell, talks about how the company's strategy for the use of professional services firms is determined by the overall corporate drive for a more global approach. In turn, working with suppliers which themselves have global organisations helps Shell get greater consistency and reinforces the strategy (see pages 53–5).

Table 5.1 shows some typical organisational strategies and some of the purchasing responses that work well in terms of their alignment with those strategies. Getting this alignment right is fundamental to effective purchasing.

However, two other aspects of the wider organisation need to be considered: its structure and culture.

Structure has a number of dimensions. Geographic is an important one,

Table 5.1 **Purchasing responses to organisational strategy**

	Typical strategy	*Appropriate purchasing response*
General industrial/services firms	Profit maximisation Steady growth	Focus on cost saving Combine with good key supplier relationships, risk management, etc A "balanced" approach
Firms with "innovation/ uniqueness" focus	Rapid revenue and market share growth Create and develop new markets	Supply chain partnerships Support mergers and acquisitions Protect critical intellectual property
Public-sector bodies	Public service Protect politicians from bad publicity	Supplier-related risk management Improve supplier delivery performance
Firms in financial difficulties	Financial survival Retain market confidence	Urgent cost savings Cash flow Supply continuity in key areas
High-profile branded goods/ sensitive public-sector bodies	Build and protect image and awareness	Corporate social responsibility Effective supplier management

but organisations can be organised around products, reflecting the range of goods or services produced, or follow a customer or market design, for example a global division selling to financial services organisations. Complex organisations may have matrix structures reflecting more than one dimension, perhaps a combination of a geographical and a product-based structure. Purchasing approaches must take all this into account. Seeking to buck the system rarely works – for example, trying to impose a highly controlled and regimented category management approach with global suppliers in an organisation that runs on a localised, product-line basis.

Managers who try to impose controls that run counter to the culture and style of their organisation generally do not last long, and so, in deciding the purchasing approach, the following needs to be considered:

- ◪ Is the culture short-term, driven by quarterly profit? Or, as in the case of some large family-owned businesses such as the Mars Corporation, does it look at issues over a period of 10–20 years, or even longer?
- ◪ Is the culture aggressive or supportive?
- ◪ What is the attitude to risk? Is it approached positively with a "bet the business" culture? Or is the organisation deeply risk averse?
- ◪ Is power concentrated in a few hands, or does the organisation work in a democratic and dispersed manner?
- ◪ Is the organisation highly structured with well-defined roles and rules, or freewheeling and loose? Is it paternalistic or laissez-faire?

Such factors are an important determinant of which types of purchasing approaches will succeed and whether a rigidly structured system for using suppliers is more or less likely to work than a looser approach.

A flexible approach

When change occurs, whether externally or internally driven (perhaps through the appointment of a new CEO), it is crucial that functional leaders review their approach to see if it is still aligned with the wider situation. Purchasing, like every function, must be sensitive to such changes in the corporate strategy and landscape. There are many examples of organisations that are highly focused on growth and market share needing to change direction quickly in response to market or economic shifts. The descent into recession during 2008 led many firms to move to a "survival strategy" that involved cutting costs, reducing stocks and other emergency financial measures.

In such cases, purchasing can play a crucial role in helping to sustain an organisation. Indeed, some people believe that the function thrives in times of economic difficulty, and it is certainly true that some approaches that a purchasing team might struggle to introduce in good times (limiting the use of consultants, for instance) become easier to implement in more difficult ones. The market may also be more amenable to aggressive purchasing approaches, although some types of professional services, such as legal services and specialist consulting relating to turnarounds or bankruptcy, thrive during a downturn.

But there are dangers if purchasing does not respond to a change in strategic direction quickly and appropriately enough, as is illustrated by the case of a large global firm which went through a period of growth in the late 1990s on the back of the dotcom boom, deregulation and globalisation. Revenue grew dramatically, acquisition followed acquisition, and up went the share price and staff numbers. The company took pride in its "leading-edge" purchasing function, headed by a director who was well respected in the purchasing profession. But there was little real governance over expenditure, and the heads of the operating companies only involved the purchasing department occasionally, in other words when they wanted to. Professional services were also not high on the purchasing team's agenda. The operating companies used consultants extensively in areas such as technology development, global market analysis and acquisitions. Money was no object: in a "war for consulting talent" in the industry at the time the leading consultants were engaged and fees of $10,000 a day were paid for senior partners with relevant industry experience.

But in 2000 the world changed: the dotcom boom came to a dramatic end and the company had to consolidate and retrench. Senior managers left and were replaced with pragmatic cost-cutters, including a new chief finance officer. But the purchasing director continued with "nice to have" initiatives and did not tighten control over costs. The new CFO soon became concerned about the lack of control of external costs and the unstructured nature of some important contracts, including those for professional services areas. The "$10,000-a-day consultant" became a source of embarrassment rather than pride. The purchasing director left and was replaced by an interim manager who, although perhaps less skilled in some ways, knew what was needed in the changed environment the firm now faced: cost cutting, spending controls and regularising contracts.

As a result the firm came through the crisis, and a new permanent purchasing director achieved the balanced approach the firm needed in the early years of the new millennium.

The importance of aligning the purchasing approach with the business strategy is reflected in Kristine Moore's account of how the purchasing approach has been developed at Shell.

Royal Dutch Shell

Kristine Moore's job as global head of indirect purchasing at Shell takes her from Houston to London and The Hague in the Netherlands. She has to oversee the company's $10 billion annual "indirect" expenditure with third parties, of which $1 billion is spent on professional services.

Moore has an unusual background for a senior purchasing leader. She worked initially for IBM, rising to a position where she managed IBM's account with Shell. After a spell in a dotcom company around the millennium, she was headhunted by Shell to work for the chief information officer. "He wanted someone to manage his supply base, and thought someone who had been one of his largest vendors was well placed to do that," she explains. Along with the vendor management role she inherited IT procurement. Not sure at first that this was the direction she wanted her career to take, she discovered that she thoroughly enjoyed purchasing, and in 2007 she was asked to manage all global indirect purchasing, including professional services, travel and a range of other categories as well as IT.

How did she find the move into purchasing?

I found we had some good people but generally they were a little narrow. They need to have the ability to put themselves in the shoes of the sales person across the negotiating table. But often they just haven't had the training that the sales people get.

Having been on both sides of the fence, Moore also knows that the ability to analyse internal customers' requirements is crucial:

We have to understand the business needs. We don't lead with our mandate or by imposing a process; we start with the view that we're here to help senior managers run their businesses.

Backed by investment Shell has been making in supplier management as a whole, Moore hired people with sales experience to bolster her team:

Our aim has been to coach our vendors' sales people to deliver, not sell. I will talk to their CEOs about their goals and targets if necessary to make sure they are aligned to our agenda. They need to bring good ideas to the table, not just try and sell us more.

Unlike Exxon, its largest competitor, Shell is extremely decentralised. There is business, geographical and functional reporting, working through complex matrix arrangements. But Shell is seeking to improve performance and operate more consistently around the world. Business strategy is highly focused on these aims, and functional strategies in areas such as IT and purchasing are aligned to the wider objectives. For instance, until recently Shell had 200 enterprise resource planning (ERP) systems; there is now a move to consolidate these, with SAP business management software as the chosen technology.

To support Shell's strategic agenda as well as to improve purchasing value, the purchasing team manages all the expenditure for functions such as IT and HR on a global basis. For instance, major IT and management consulting providers need to be able to support the global IT delivery programmes. Moore and her team have therefore put in place global "master service agreements", leading to consolidation of spend. As a result, 90% of the consulting spend in the finance area is now through three major suppliers. At the same time, the team is sensitive to market realities: there are no real global providers in some subcategories within the professional services portfolio, so regional agreements will be put in place in such cases. The overall direction, however, is towards global. Moore says:

We allow legacy contracts to continue; but new agreements should be as globally applicable as possible.

We have three stages of the sourcing process: stakeholder engagement, sourcing strategy and contract management. It sounds straightforward, but just the stakeholder engagement stage can be as simple as herding the proverbial cats. It's worth the effort, though. In our experience, price negotiations rarely account for more than 20% of the value we add (which we calculate as the cost of an assignment if we hadn't been involved, less its cost when we are involved), whereas managing demand and challenging the specification of an assignment each account for about 40% of our value. Rates are important – hence the benchmarking effort we're currently undertaking – but managing the internal dimensions of demand and specification can drive more value for Shell. Demand management is business-led, with the corporate purchasing team assisting and enabling; specification is a shared responsibility; and price is purchasing led. We challenge the business in terms of demand. Do we really need these services? Can we afford them? Can we source the requirement and necessary skills internally? Governance is very important in order to enforce this.

When it comes to specification, the purchasing team can challenge who and what is needed. Moore considers consulting requirements in terms of what the real need is:

I think of it as head, eyes, or arms and legs. "Head" is real thinking, intellectual capital work. "Eyes" is the ability to review what we are doing, comment critically or benchmark what we are doing. "Arms and legs" are the times when what we really need are smart people to work under our direction.

Her team will review whether the requirement is truly strategic. Does it need consulting services or can it be done by contract labour? What expertise is really needed? To assist this process, Shell has rationalised its definitions of capabilities and categories; for example, there are now just five defined service lines for finance consulting, based on recognised industry domains.

Good planning can also help with the specification stage. Moore's team will challenge the level of seniority that the internal client may think they need: "We want to pay for the work, not the person," says Moore. Contracts are based on deliverables wherever possible, rather than time and materials. Contracting in phases can help: putting commercial checkpoints in place, and ensuring there is transferability between phases so that there can be further competition at each stage rather than being locked into one supplier. The governance regime supports purchasing involvement, and Moore ensures that internal clients understand the difference between an investment proposal, sign-off based on return on investment (ROI) and the commercial proposal, which drives their market price and requires purchasing involvement.

Prices are managed by detailed rate cards, which come under a global master service agreement. Prices are agreed by service line, grade level of the individual consultant and location. Is there a danger of losing negotiating leverage given the way in which Shell has rationalised supplier numbers? Moore thinks not; smart purchasing people can maintain competitive tension in markets with only three or four suppliers. Offshoring is another negotiating lever, and contracts contain annual benchmarking provisions, with rates calibrated every 6–12 months using external benchmarks. Detailed regional benchmarking is carried out in many category areas, and preferred supplier lists are refreshed regularly so that suppliers do not get complacent.

"We aim," Moore sums up, "to bring commercial objectivity into an area that has traditionally been subjective."

6 Requirements and specifications

Martin Webb worked as a chief purchasing officer (CPO) for many years, including for French, German, and British telecommunications firms. He says:

> Organisations often fail to identify the root causes of the issues before they engage consultants, or really understand what they want them to do. That means that the requirements are not well defined; or the consultants arrive to find that the climate is not right for them to succeed. They may not have the right information, the right level of access to people, or the right internal resources. All this stems from a lack of clarity around what the organisation actually wants them to do. In one of my CPO roles, we developed a toolkit for budget holders, not just around engaging consultants, but also covering the pre-engagement phase, helping them to think about defining the problem, and structuring the requirement before we approached the market.

But professional services firms don't always help themselves, in Webb's opinion:

> They're often not very good at segmenting their own services or at identifying what they do that really adds value and what is more of a "commodity" product, and targeting and marketing appropriately. As purchasing people get smarter and more perceptive about these markets, suppliers will also need to ensure they understand their own offerings.

Why are requirements and specifications so important within the overall purchasing process? Simply because they define – as exactly as possible – what it is that the buyer wants the supplier to do. Getting this right makes it possible to choose a supplier who will achieve the desired outcome and meet the needs of the purchasing organisation. Getting it wrong will, almost inevitably, lead to an outcome that is not what is wanted and may lead to disaster.

This chapter looks at who should write a specification and what should go into it. It outlines the different types of specification ("brand", input-based, technical and performance specifications) and how to draw up specifications for framework agreements, as well as for simple assignments.

The *Concise Oxford English Dictionary* defines a specification as "a detailed description of the construction, workmanship, materials etc of work done or to be done" and a requirement as "a need; depended on for success or fulfilment". A specification describes fully or partially how we expect our requirements to be met. Thus, "We need someone to come in and write a strategy to expand our business into Canada" is a requirement, but "the person needs to have an MBA from a top business school, five years' minimum consulting experience and be able to deliver the work by the end of September" is a (partial) specification.

In professional services the terms requirements and specifications are used fairly interchangeably, but they both need to be clearly communicated to suppliers or potential suppliers for important reasons:

◪ Statements of requirements or specifications allow suppliers to assess whether they can do the work. If they can, such statements help them put forward a proposal or tender which describes how they will meet the specification or requirement and their fitness to carry out the assignment.
◪ Where suppliers are competing to win the contract to carry out the assignment, these statements form the common basis on which they bid.
◪ In many cases, they will form at least part of the eventual contractual relationship.

Unfortunately, the definitions of requirements and specifications within professional services purchasing are often weak. "Get me a consultant – I need some help" is not untypical. This is obviously not a statement of requirements on which sensible supplier selection can be based. Where consultants or other professionals are engaged without a clear idea of what it is they are required to do, the result will be poor outcomes and dissatisfied customers (and suppliers). Effort put in at this stage will be repaid many times.

Although this chapter focuses on requirements for specific pieces of work or assignments, much of the information is also relevant in cases where a purchaser is seeking to appoint suppliers to a framework or approved supplier list.

You are not buying pencils

One of the most frequent complaints from services providers is that purchasers of professional services use much the same approach as they do for buying pencils. It is a major irritation among professional services firms and can lead to poor supplier selection.

Requirements must be relevant to the particular circumstances, whereas purchasers often do no more than cut and paste from an existing and inappropriate set of purchasing documents designed for a different type of purchase. Specifications, tender or contract documents are then presented to suppliers in a language more suitable to purchasing equipment or raw materials. References to delivery locations, after-sales service or quality inspections are not unheard of. Some services firms have been asked to supply their own tools and safety equipment: one management consulting firm was asked to provide its own oxygen cylinders and protective clothing.

The requirement or specification must take into account the type of service being bought and should reflect its complexity, level of risk, contract value and duration. If the need is urgent but with limited cost or risk ("we need some quick legal advice on this fairly straightforward deal now"), a short but precise specification may be appropriate. And on occasions urgency may justify the engagement of professional services support before the requirements are well defined. But if the assignment is expected to run for two years, cost millions of dollars and have a major impact on the buying organisation, it is clearly essential that a detailed description of requirements is drawn up.

Who is responsible for the requirements or specification?

For most single assignments (rather than frameworks), it is the user of the professional service who is best able to draw up the requirements and specification. Purchasing staff can provide useful input in terms of how requirements can best be presented to suppliers to encourage competition and strong proposals, and how to structure the evaluation process and related documents. But users of the service are best placed to articulate the core business needs.

Purchasing teams can also play a useful role in challenging the thinking of users. Do they really need a consultant from a top-flight strategic firm? Would an experienced independent consultant fit the bill better? Equally, pushing users towards a generic solution, perhaps because of a desire that they use the standard framework of suppliers, when they really have a specialist requirement, rarely helps internal relationships or produces a successful outcome.

The user and the purchasing manager should work together and agree the requirements and how to present them to the potential suppliers in a manner that will maximise the chances of success and value for money. This is, after all, the objective of both users and purchasing staff.

What should go into a specification?

As stated earlier, the terms specification and requirements are often used interchangeably. What matters is the totality of information provided to potential suppliers to help them propose how they will carry out the assignment.

Apart from defining the services required, a specification will often include or have appended other details, especially where it is to provide the basis for a competitive bidding process:

- **Additional information.** Documentation may be incorporated that forms part of the wider briefing for potential suppliers, aimed at helping them respond to the requirement.
- **A draft contract.** This may support the specification directly – for example, by defining precisely what is meant by "promptly" in the phrase "supplier must provide services promptly" in the specification.
- **Metrics.** Details of any potential service level agreements or key performance indicators (whether or not they form part of the formal contract) will be useful to suppliers in terms of their understanding of the requirements. They will also play an important role in the suppliers' pricing of the work.

The specification may also contain what might be termed background information relating to the specific requirement of the buying organisation. This could include the following:

- **Operational information.** For example, a list of the buying organisation's sites to which services may need to be delivered, or other details that aid understanding of what is needed.
- **Security.** For example, data security or restrictions on the staff who can carry out the work, handle sensitive information, and so on.
- **Standards.** For example, generic industry standards that suppliers must meet such as ISO accreditation, or standards that are more specific to the client.

Types of specification

There are four main types of specification for expressing what the buyer wants as clearly as possible.

"Brand" specification

When buying goods, it is common to specify the brand you want. Although it is less common to do so when buying services, many professional services firms work hard to build brand recognition to give themselves a marketing edge.

When buying professional services, brand specification may make sense; for example, a legal issue may be so critical that it is appropriate to specify the world's best lawyer in that field. But in general, specifying a particular firm or an individual not only narrows your options (to one) but also makes it harder to get value for money because there is no competition to that one.

Input-based specification

This defines the inputs, the type of resources, to be provided, rather than the outputs. The requirement might be, "We want a project manager for four weeks starting next Monday". In most cases, however, this will be elaborated upon by some constraints or with more detail, such as what experience and qualifications are required. The main problem with input-based specifications is that they are rarely precise. The statement "We want a lawyer experienced in commercial property to support us over the next few months in our acquisition of new premises" may give some idea of what is required, but how experienced is experienced? What kind of premises are being acquired? Are the issues involved strategic or purely tactical? Is "a few months" three months or six? Imprecision is unhelpful: potential suppliers may not know whether to put forward a partner or a junior, or whether the person is going to be needed for a few hours a month or virtually full time.

Technical specification

The difference between an input-based specification and a technical specification is largely one of detail. Here is part of the technical specification for a well-known item of consumer electronics, taken directly from the manufacturer's website:

> *H.264 video, up to 1.5 Mbps, 640 by 480 pixels, 30 frames per second, Low-Complexity version of the H.264 Baseline Profile with AAC-LC audio up to 160*

Kbps, 48kHz, stereo audio in .m4v, .mp4, and .mov file formats; H.264 video, up to 2.5 Mbps, 640 by 480 pixels, 30 frames per second, Baseline Profile up to Level 3.0 with AAC-LC audio up to 160 Kbps, 48kHz, stereo audio in .m4v, .mp4, and .mov file formats; MPEG-4 video, up to 2.5 Mbps, 640 by 480 pixels, 30 frames per second, Simple Profile with AAC-LC audio up to 160 Kbps, 48kHz, stereo audio in .m4v, .mp4, and .mov file formats

Technical specifications have the benefit of clarity. To the right person, this sort of description makes it clear what they are buying; it would be just as clear to a supplier if it were given as a purchasing specification. What a buyer defines in a specification should be what it gets; if it is not, it will know straightaway. But it does have drawbacks. Ironically, although it looks different from a branded specification, it is so prescriptive that it may restrict the number of suppliers who can bid, or the range of solutions possible. No other MP3 player may be able to meet this specification, but that does not necessarily mean that no other player would meet the needs of the buyer.

Services are different from goods, but similar principles apply. If the specification reflects too closely specific technical attributes associated with a particular professional services provider, or proprietary products that it offers, it will be difficult for other firms to compete. A specification might be that the law firm being chosen must have offices in over 50 countries; that may be a necessary criterion for the selection, but the purchaser must understand that such a requirement will reduce competition dramatically. The purchasing team need to be aware of this – and that although user input into a specification is desirable if not always crucial, a user can skew the selection and constrain the competitive process by being too precise.

Performance specification

Performance specifications give potential suppliers the opportunity to specify how the work will be carried out. It is well suited to the purchasing of professional services where experienced suppliers often have a deeper understanding of what is needed than the purchaser. It also opens the market to more potential suppliers than the other three types of specifications.

Performance specifications can be based on either outputs or outcome, depending on the circumstances and, most importantly, what is practical and achievable:

◪ An output-based specification focuses on what is desired from a service in business terms, rather than giving a detailed technical specification of how it is to be provided. This gives suppliers an opportunity to propose their own potentially innovative solutions, perhaps ones the purchasing organisation had not considered. Such a specification would ask for a consulting report on the effectiveness of the procurement function, with particular focus on five or six aspects of that function. It would not define exactly how the work had to be carried out.

◪ An outcome-based specification is concerned with the delivery of a result, such as winning a legal case or an improvement in the performance of part of the business. The concept is attractive, but in practice it is often easier for a buyer to define a desired outcome than it is for a supplier to price a bid or to know whether or not to accept the risk involved in committing to the delivery of a specific result. Few lawyers, for example, would accept a "no win no fee" risk, because the result cannot be guaranteed and assessing the workload needed to maximise the chances of success is difficult. However, it has been used successfully: when the UK government invited organisations to tender for services to get long-term unemployed and disabled people into jobs, it focused on the outcomes it wanted to achieve. They were defined in terms of the target proportion of individuals referred to the organisations who found jobs, and the length of time they would sustain those jobs. With those objectives clearly defined, payment has been strongly linked to the success of suppliers in achieving the desired outcomes.

As a general rule, performance specifications should be used where feasible, not least because they allow suppliers to give their view of the best way of achieving the output/outcome and to put forward an efficient proposal. They encourage innovation, and give new suppliers scope to challenge incumbent suppliers and assumptions about how things are done.

Combining types of specification

It may make sense to combine the different types of specification, as the case of an engineering multinational illustrates. The company faced a claim that a piece of equipment it sold for several million dollars was faulty. The claimant sought the return of the purchase price plus substantial damages for consequential losses. The engineering company believed that the equipment was fine and that the buyer had refused to take its advice on installation, installed it wrongly and failed to maintain it properly, resulting in a breakdown after just six months. It needed professional help in fighting the claim and had to formulate a specification that could be given to legal firms invited to pitch for the work.

A solely outcome-based approach – "tell us how you would win this case" – would not work as no firm would take on the entire risk of losing the case, or be able to price doing so. A purely input-based or technical specification would have been equally problematic, in that it was impossible to know how much work was likely, whether the case would come to trial and so on. And the engineering company did not have the knowledge to specify a particular firm or individual (the branded option).

In the event, the multinational drew up an initial output-based specification for the delivery by a certain date of a report in which the lawyers would analyse the position and prepare a paper laying out the crucial points of the case, the likely costs and the likelihood of success. Exactly how the legal firm would put that report together was left open, although it was asked to describe its approach and methodology in its proposal. The engineering company also provided rough guidance on the expected cost so that potential suppliers would not make wildly different assumptions about the money available for the work. A second input-based specification was drawn up to cover the likely need for further, unspecified legal advice, to be given by a lawyer of particular seniority, qualifications and background, who was to be available as and when required. Potential suppliers could then give a "day-rate" they would charge for a named individual.

Specifications for frameworks

When a framework or preferred list of suppliers (see Chapter 10 for further details) is to be selected to meet a range of needs over a period of time, the specification may be very different from that for a single assignment. If the aim is to appoint several suppliers, a more generic set of requirements may be used, at least in the initial stages, in the absence of details about what will be required from each supplier.

So rather than assignment-specific outputs or inputs, the requirements defined for potential framework suppliers may focus more on aspects such as:

- the general capabilities or experience of the professional services firms;
- the specific capabilities required of individuals within the firms;
- general aspects of service required from the firm;
- assignment management requirements, including quality, account management or management reporting processes.

Reviewing specifications

Developing a specification is often seen as a one-off activity, carried out at the beginning of the supplier selection process or when engaging a supplier. But for assignments of any length, it should be reviewed regularly. Is it still valid? Does it need to be renewed? Should it be revised? What is the process for renewal or revision? The initial concept should anticipate and allow for the possibility of revision at a later date. Contracts should be designed with the flexibility to allow reasonable changes in requirements throughout the life of the contract, through clear change control mechanisms. This is discussed further in Chapter 18.

Ashley Unwin's comments (see below) highlight the need for purchasing staff to understand fully the business and users' needs if they are to contribute properly to specifying work and engaging suppliers.

From EMI to PricewaterhouseCoopers

Ashley Unwin's career has taken him from Andersen and Deloitte's consulting practices, where he was head of the strategy and change practices, to private equity, and now back to consulting, taking over PwC's consulting practice in the UK. During his time working for Terra Firma, a private equity firm run by Guy Hands, he was CEO of EMI in the UK, Ireland and North America, a position that gave him a broad view of the strengths and weaknesses of procurement departments. He says:

It's obvious why the procurement process, and that of professional services in particular, had to change in most big organisations. At EMI, a wide variety of people had the authority to spend considerable amounts on what is in essence an intangible service. We needed to monitor and manage this and all other expenditure if we were to ensure we were spending our money wisely.

But Unwin also recognises that it is all too easy for a procurement team to focus on their internal objectives and to lose sight of what the organisation is trying to achieve:

Procurement departments sometimes fail to understand the strategic and commercial drivers of their organisation. They often revert to a checklist, which doesn't always take account of what is most important.

A significant implication of this, Unwin believes, is that while all suppliers are treated equally, this devalues the importance of relationships in a professional services context and ignores the fact that a supplier can play a critical role over and above the services it has been asked to deliver:

The role of the professional adviser is to support and challenge. If you make the procurement process too sterile, then a proposal that simply ticks the boxes and/or a good sales pitch will carry the day. You can't evaluate a relationship with a checklist. If a board is facing difficult challenges, then they need people who can understand their context, what they are trying to achieve and foresee the challenges ahead. If you're buying a service, you need to understand who's good, what the market rate is and the kind of people you want to engage to do it. If you don't understand this, especially in a harsh economic environment, you'll buy services from someone who ticks all the boxes but maybe is not best placed to help.

Going to PwC has made it even clearer to Unwin where procurement departments can still fall short:

Procurement professionals who understand professional services are still comparatively rare; more often they can become a wedge between suppliers and their clients. Although that makes them more objective, they might find it difficult to make the connection back to what's actually needed, the strategic context for a piece of work, for instance. They don't necessarily understand why a particular piece of work is so important, but might see it in isolation and ignore the value a supplier which knows their organisation may be able to bring. We end up debating points with them which we know their internal customers think are important but which they don't recognise as adding value.

Unwin believes that there is a need for more intelligent buyers of professional services. "They've made themselves subordinate to a process which ultimately makes them less intelligent," he argues. Seeing the situation as both a user and a supplier, Unwin believes that the procurement function needs to move out of the back office in much the same way that financial and human resource teams have done in recent years:

A forward-thinking finance function will know that its future status depends on not being perceived to be focused just on reporting past events but also on pulling together the management information required to foresee events. Procurement teams have to take a similar step, presenting themselves less as people forcing adherence to checklists and more as business partners who play a strategic role in acquiring the resources their organisation needs to do business. Procurement teams have much more to add to the business than simply beating a few suppliers down on price.

7 Acting as an intermediary

Jason Busch of Spend Matters, one of the leading purchasing and supply chain websites in the United States, and Azul Partners, comments:

> Involvement of purchasing staff in professional services is still patchy in the United States. It is a continuum of influence. In many organisations, purchasing gets involved in interim labour deals. At the next level, they may be involved in marketing and print services. Then we see those cases where purchasing is "dabbling" in consulting or legal spend, without really understanding what they are doing. Only the very best purchasing teams are really getting to grips with these categories, but where they are, their approach goes far beyond conventional "doing deals", into sophisticated demand and contract management processes for instance.

So how can purchasing people and departments have a successful impact on the purchasing of professional services in their organisation? A good working relationship between a purchasing department and its internal customers is essential. The links between the purchasing team, the end-user and the supplier need to be balanced if they are to work together effectively.

A three-way relationship

In most organisations there are three main participants in the purchasing process:

- the supplier of the goods and services;
- the purchaser, who puts in place the contractual arrangement;
- the user of the goods and services within the purchasing organisation.

The roles they play are interdependent (see Figure 7.1). Users may buy goods or services direct from a supplier or they may rely on their organisation's procurement department (the purchaser) to negotiate the contract and price. Purchasers are also there to help users identify the

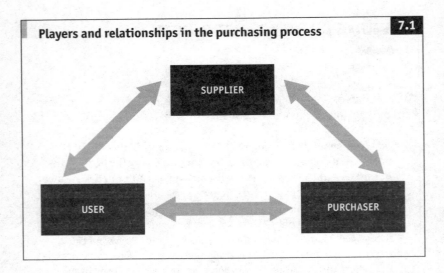

Players and relationships in the purchasing process   7.1

most appropriate supplier and to work with suppliers to ensure they provide good value for money. Suppliers, of course, deal with both sides.

When, as is the case in most large organisations, there is a separate purchasing function, this creates an inherent tension. The purchasing team will almost always be focused on value for money, which often involves cutting costs or consolidating suppliers and achieving economies of scale. However, users will be focused on their business objectives and will resent what they consider to be attempts by the procurement team to restrict their choice of supplier and prevent them doing their job.

When users control the budget they are more likely to see the procurement function as an obstacle; when the procurement department controls expenditure, perhaps because there is an organisation-wide budget for a particular good or service, it may want to deter users from spending what it regards as its money. Suppliers will understandably gravitate to whoever controls the budget, but if the budget holder is not the user, they may be torn between delivering a good service and trying to satisfy the procurement department's desire to keep costs down. Where the cost/quality debate between users and purchasers has not been resolved, suppliers will be in the invidious position of trying – and failing – to keep both sides happy.

This three-way tension is particularly acute in the procurement of professional services. Finding a way to resolve it is essential if an organisation is achieve the best overall results, allowing the users to buy the services they need and the procurement team to focus on value for money.

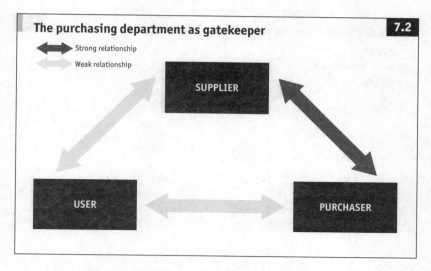

The purchasing department as gatekeeper — 7.2

Strong relationship
Weak relationship

SUPPLIER

USER

PURCHASER

Gatekeeper or faithful servant?

"Gatekeepers" are those who concentrate on the purchasing process, compliance and policy. They see their job as protecting the organisation against the users who, given half a chance, would spend their organisation's money foolishly or even beyond their authority. Purchasing gatekeepers make every effort to put in place policies that give them the upper hand over users of professional services; they establish lists of suppliers beyond which users may not stray; they seek to lead on negotiations, choose the supplier and dictate terms and conditions.

For gatekeepers, the relationship between themselves and their suppliers is what matters most, especially during the contracting phase (see Figure 7.2). Even when a contract is in place and work starts, they will keep an eye on things, trying to ensure that users and suppliers do not get too close, as that might threaten their authority and control.

A decade or two ago, many purchasing departments aspired to the "gatekeeper" model. Control over spending on procurement was sought, albeit often unsuccessfully. This lack of success was most marked in the purchase of professional services because gatekeepers found it particularly hard to infiltrate the close relationships that had traditionally existed between users and professional advisers, often at senior levels. The result was impressively thick process manuals, preferred supplier lists and policies. By contrast, practical compliance was poor on the part of users, who tended to take a dim view of purchasing staff.

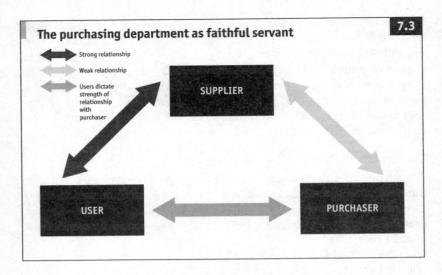

The clear flaws in the gatekeeper approach led to a shift towards better user engagement in the shape of a "faithful servant" model (see Figure 7.3).

The danger of this approach is that it can lead to purchasing people who are helpful but do not challenge users or get as much value as they could from professional services spending. Faithful servants see their role as enablers, supporting users in the procurement of professional services. The purchasing team may assist, but only where users want them to. They may be involved in selecting suppliers and setting out basic terms and conditions, but always at the request of the users. If the users decide to manage the procurement process themselves, faithful servants will politely withdraw.

In the procurement of professional services, the faithful servant approach may lead to chaotic, poorly controlled spending patterns. Lack of governance over the process, and lack of objectivity in selecting suppliers and negotiating contracts, can lead to supplier choice based purely on friendships and personal prejudices. Suppliers find they can economically exploit the buying organisation. Selling becomes a matter of developing strong relationships with decision-makers, rather than providing the best value business solution.

Despite the drawbacks, there are occasions when either a gatekeeper or a faithful servant approach makes sense. When an international bank found itself the subject of an unexpected and sudden takeover bid, it was interesting how quickly all the control measures that the purchasing director had been suggesting for years were immediately implemented. By contrast, an organisation which is financially secure and seeking to expand will need faithful servants who will help rather than hinder the pursuit of growth. This explains why purchasing people have struggled in sectors such as investment banking; if bond dealers are keen on a new piece of software that they believe will help them hugely increase profits, they are unlikely to wait months for the purchasing department to investigate the options.

Constructive relationships

The success of a professional services assignment depends on the relationships between users, purchasers and suppliers being balanced and constructive. The appropriate policies, process and governance to manage professional services spending must be in place; the needs of the user must be recognised by both the purchaser and the supplier; and, whoever takes the lead role, both the purchaser and the user must be involved in selecting and engaging the supplier.

Table 7.1 **Purchasing roles**

	Drivers	Process focus	Purchasing style
Gatekeeper	Control demand Procurement power to drive value Mistrust of users	Strong policies Tight authorisation Limited range of suppliers	Enforce policies with users Purchasers lead process Dominant interface with market
Faithful servant	Decentralisation Speed of action Delegated management style	Limited controls on users Loose procurement process "Open sourcing" from the market	Helpful but subservient to users Users lead process Market interface as defined by users
Business partner	Good governance combined with business focus Balance between local autonomy and central control	Clear policies and authorisations Collaborative working internally and with suppliers	Manage the policy and work positively with users Joint approach to process and market interface

The relationships change during the purchasing process. Once the contract is up and running, the links between user and supplier will be stronger, but this close working relationship will be allied to effective contract and supplier management, with the purchasing team continuing to play an important role.

The role that balances or combines the best of the gatekeeper and faithful servant roles can be described as that of "business partner" (see Table 7.1). This balanced approach, in which the purchasing team plays the role of a business partner, has clear advantages. The purchasing department achieves control over spending, enabling it to look for value through aggregation, careful selection of suppliers and effective management of contractual deliverables. But users also feel that their role is recognised; they have a major input into supplier selection and management, and suppliers recognise that ultimately they have to deliver the desired outcome.

The skills required of a business partner

There are four types of skills a business partner needs when buying professional services:

- **Market knowledge.** Procurement people who are not up to speed on the range and variety of professional services firms will always be on the back foot when dealing with users. Knowing which firms deliver which services and what their strengths, weaknesses and pricing structures are earns them the right to discuss the choice of firm with users and to challenge their assumptions. Understanding overall trends allows them to portray themselves in a more strategic light, as people who are experts rather than administrators. Process is important, but a business partner will seek to place it in the context of the challenges of buying a particular professional service, whereas a gatekeeper will see it as an end in itself and a faithful servant will treat it as an obstacle to be circumvented.
- **Internal intelligence.** Business partners also need to have a handle on patterns of demand within their own organisation. This can range from knowing, for example, that a different business unit recently hired a consulting team to look at the same issue to a clear sense of the organisation's strategic objectives and priorities and whether, for instance, it makes sense to implement a new IT system now. Professional services firms thrive on the inability of business units or departments within an organisation to exchange

information effectively, and a central role of the procurement team is to make sure that relevant information is shared and not duplicated.

- **Communication skills.** With more facts at their fingertips, business partners are better able to explain the reasons for policies and procedures. Many preferred supplier lists fail, not because the wrong firms have been selected, but because no one in the procurement team has taken the trouble to explain why they have been chosen. Indeed, the whole idea of a list encourages procurement people to provide the bare minimum of information: the emphasis falls on compliance rather than giving users the information they need to make a sensible choice.

- **The ability to see projects in their entirety.** One reason procurement people are often asked to sort out the paperwork on done deals is an almost exclusive focus on the buying process; hence users have seen no point in involving them before coming to a decision on what service is needed and who should provide it. The role of the business partner, however, starts earlier, by helping users analyse what value they think an external firm will add and why the resources required cannot be found internally. It also finishes later: when procurement people act as business partners, their remit extends to include monitoring progress and evaluating supplier performance.

A business partner must also have self-confidence. Poor market information, lack of internal support and a holier-than-thou attitude among some professional services firms can make procurement people apologetic. When resented by users and suppliers, they sometimes try to be unobtrusive (albeit efficient) that they become invisible. Having the self-confidence to communicate a deep knowledge of the professional services market and the ability to add value at all stages of a project's life is essential if procurement people are to get others to take them seriously.

The experiences of Guy Allen at Fujitsu (see below) highlight how important it is that purchasing people have the confidence to fulfil their role as business partner.

Fujitsu Services

Guy Allen is familiar with the tightrope a buyer walks, particularly on professional services. After purchasing roles at IBM, Ford and GlaxoSmithKline, he became head of procurement at Abbey, both before and after its takeover by Banco Santander, Spain's largest bank. He is now director of sourcing and supply services at Fujitsu Services. Therein lies an additional layer of complexity: he is responsible for buying not only for Fujitsu Services but also for its clients. Allen says:

> *What makes it different from many purchasing jobs is that we effectively have two roles. We buy goods and services for internal use, but we also buy on behalf of customers, and we support our sales teams in their bid activities. Major outsourcing bids, for example, generally contain an element of subcontractor costs – and it's my team that provide the input to ensure we bid accurately but as competitively as possible.*

This creates some specific challenges: the range and variety of specialist skills required make it impossible to take a one-size-fits-all approach to professional services and difficult to achieve the volume discounts an organisation as big as Fujitsu might expect. It also means Allen's team have to know their subject and be able to work closely with the users.

What does this mean in terms of the role purchasing staff play? Are they gatekeepers applying strong policies or faithful servants supporting their internal customers? Allen says:

> *We're not into the old style "thou shalt not buy" role for purchasing. But equally I don't think we should apologise for our involvement. I tell my team they have a right to a seat at the table when it comes to purchasing decisions. The purchasing profession has got a little over-excited about "selling" our services internally; we are not selling in the sense of giving people the option whether or not they engage with purchasing. The concept of purchasing being a "business partner" sounds good but it's not always clearly defined: I want my people to be confident about applying the processes, principles and policies we have in Fujitsu. In some ways, it would be easier if we were simple gatekeepers, but ultimately less effective.*
>
> *My team have to support users and demonstrate they are adding value: it's how we build our reputation and it takes time to do. They add value through their knowledge of the market and suppliers, and their ability to run professional purchasing and contracting processes. For instance, I expect my team to know more about their suppliers than the suppliers know about us. That's a tough challenge. We also make it clear that we're not here to tell them which supplier to use, but to make sure we've a strong, rational decision-making process that supports our overall goals. I find that sensible users want*

our involvement: as well as the real added value, it gives them assurance
and an audit trail around the way they are spending the company's money.
Often, it is the purchasing team who see different activities going on around
the organisation and bring disparate parts together, and senior managers
appreciate this type of facilitation.

As far as the purchase of professional services is concerned, Allen highlights two
main challenges in making the relationship between users and purchasing people
work. The first is the level at which his team has to operate:

Most of the expenditure in this area is driven by pretty senior people, and my
team has to be able to work a couple of levels up the organisation in terms of
hierarchy. I have a young manager going into a meeting with the chief executive
to discuss a big consulting contract. I know she'll do a good job: my role is to
give her the confidence to do it.

As is so often the case, senior directors may not want to be limited to the firms on
Fujitsu's preferred supplier list, but that is something Allen prefers to work with, not
against:

If a senior executive wants do something outside the norm, we have to realise
there's probably a good reason. I don't, for instance, expect the chief executive
to let everyone in purchasing know if he is engaging a consultant to support a
possible top-secret acquisition.

Experience has also taught Allen that it is important to engage people who
may not be direct users of professional services. At Abbey, he and his team greatly
improved the way in which expenditure on legal services was managed:

It was essential to get the buy-in of Abbey's internal lawyers. Once we had
that, we could segment the market and buy the appropriate services at the
appropriate cost. There is a role for the "magic circle" lawyers, but you don't
have to use them for every standard transaction.

Success, he believes, comes down to the role his people play: dealing with senior
management professionally; offering value and assistance while being firm when it
comes to policy and process.

The second challenge is finding people who can perform this balancing act well:

I have some great people but the combination of professional and business *skills and the right character and behaviours is hard to find. The phrase I particularly like to describe what I am looking for is "intestinal fortitude". They have to be able to hold their own with suppliers and internal stakeholders – determination, tenacity, independence are key attributes.*

These are not things that are easy to learn on conventional training courses, so Fujitsu runs its own sourcing "academy", which has focused on these areas as well as the more conventional professional training:

We've won two awards from the Chartered Institute of Purchasing and Supply in the last couple of years. We're not complacent but it feels like we're moving in the right direction.

PART 3
PURCHASING APPROACHES

This section of the book moves from the more strategic issues – the relationship between an organisation as a whole and its buying team – to the more tactical.

The way in which professional services are bought and sold often challenges organisational purchasing rules. When does an important and effective working relationship become too close for its own good? Equally, how likely is it that a chief executive would be willing to expose a decision to hire a strategy consultancy for a sensitive project or an investment bank for an acquisition to the scrutiny of a purchasing department?

However, category management, an approach that has served purchasing well in other areas, can usefully be applied to professional services, although its design and implementation need careful thought. Frameworks and preferred supplier lists have their place here as well, but again need to be applied with care if they are not to create too rigid a structure for services that, by definition, have to be tailored to specific needs.

8 Governance, influence and demand management

The drive to apply good practice to the purchasing of professional services usually comes from the purchasing team. But this can only be done with the co-operation of those who have control over budgets and the final say on appointing advisers. The good intentions of a purchasing team are of little use if they come to nothing as a result of failure to get the necessary internal support and involvement.

Of all the third-party spending categories, professional services is one where co-operation between purchasers and users is crucial for success. Organisations use different terms to describe the process of getting others within an organisation on side: stakeholder management, internal politics, governance, process control. "Governance" is perhaps the most appropriate word for the formal or "hard" means by which co-operation is achieved, but informal influence, the "soft" means, is in many cases just as important.

Governance

Governance of an organisation's spending on third parties is important because, in theory at least, it clearly defines the rules. Unless people, including suppliers, understand those rules – know who does what within the overall purchasing process, who can sign off contracts and orders and so on – an organisation will be exposed to the risks of time wasting, internal arguments about responsibilities, incompetence and fraud. Well-understood rules also help reassure external stakeholders such as shareholders or taxpayers in the case of government bodies that "their" money is being spent properly.

However, just as the purchasing approach needs to align with corporate strategy (see Chapter 5), governance regimes need to be aligned with an organisation's style. A computer games company started and owned by three geeks in California will take a different approach to that of a large multinational – although even "relaxed" companies get keener on rules and policies once the original owners start delegating expenditure decisions to employees. But all organisations should have a system of purchasing governance in place that is proportionate and does not act as a bureaucratic brake on effectiveness.

Influencing techniques

Whatever system of governance exists, purchasing teams must have the ability to exercise influence over those they are there to help, including the senior managers who are often involved in commissioning professional services assignments, and who may have strong existing relationships with individual advisers or firms. This involves building constructive internal relationships and using persuasion rather than threats.

There are many influencing, or negotiating, techniques that can be used. Neuro-linguistic programming (NLP) is chiefly concerned with the relationship between successful patterns of behaviour and the subjective experiences underlying them. It has advocates in business, who use NLP techniques such as imitating the behaviour or even the physical style and position of the other party ("matching and pacing non-verbal behaviour" as it is called in NLP language) to establish rapport, gather information or influence others more successfully.

Confidence and an ability to be credible at the highest levels of an organisation are also important. Several chief procurement officers interviewed for this book talk about the need to have professional services purchasing people who can hold their own, not only with senior partners in the provider firms, but also with their own board directors. Some of those skills can be learnt; some are probably largely inherent in the personality, drive, intelligence and communication skills of the individuals.

Demand management

Neil Punwani, who has had senior roles at several consumer products companies, says:

> Of course agency costs matter. There is always an ambitious list of client projects that are not funded, and there is always pressure to do more with less. Ultimately, though, it is the responsibility of senior management to stand behind the choices they make – and that means considering added value first – not cost. We had a budget of how much we were planning to spend on a particular campaign, but the critical thing for us was how good the agency was. Sometimes we went with the cheapest alternative, sometimes the most expensive, but the first criterion was always quality. For an engagement lasting 1–2 years or more, that is a long time to

> *regret choosing the wrong partner and constantly reviewing and amending substandard work – ultimately it drains the time and energy of your whole team, and other priorities suffer. I was often surprised that agencies brought up costs or willingness to discount in initial meetings – for me this always sent the wrong signal. If the costs were high but the partner was right, we would often make the painful decision to do fewer projects but do them right.*

The best way to save money on purchasing is to buy less or nothing at all. That is what is known as demand management. In terms of professional services, it may be possible to use internal staff to carry out the work rather than engaging outsiders – perhaps staff from another business unit who have the relevant experience now needed by the client. Or it may be that careful analysis of existing information, or perhaps even previous professional services advice, reduces the need for new work.

The purchasing department's ability to manage demand depends on knowing what users are doing and when they are planning to spend money on professional services. Having a policy and a governance system that require users to involve and inform the purchasing department in processes and decisions involving expenditure will help. Kristine Moore of Shell (see page 53) uses demand management to generate real benefits. She rates it as having more influence on delivering value from professional services than price negotiation. She and her team question what users are buying and whether the assignment is necessary or appropriately defined. Policy and governance processes support this; but she highlights the need for purchasing people with strong interpersonal skills who can influence both providers and internal colleagues. Jim Hemmington of the BBC (see page 111) similarly talks about the role of his team in challenging whether users really need external support, or whether work can be done using internal resources.

Many managers are set on spending their budgets on top consultants even if they could achieve a successful outcome for half the money. It is not for purchasing people to dictate what users should be doing, but they can and should challenge budget holders' preconceptions and look at how demand can be best managed.

What to include in a purchasing policy

There are a number of aspects a purchasing policy should address, including the following:

- **Delegation levels.** How much money can people commit on behalf of the organisation? Most policies make the distinction between a financial delegation (control over a budget); and purchasing/contractual delegation (the ability to enter into a contract with a third party).
- **Who does what.** What is the role of the purchasing department and when should it be involved? Most organisations make sure that a single person cannot choose a supplier, place an order and authorise payment.
- **Frameworks.** When and how frameworks should be used.
- **Rules for tendering.** Most organisations will apply different rules for different amounts of spending. A small piece of legal advice, worth a couple of thousand dollars, may not require any formal competition or a tendering process. For greater levels of expenditure, the policy may define a particular purchasing process such as full tendering.
- **Rules for single tenders.** Organisations may specify when or whether suppliers can be engaged without any competition. This can be a sensitive issue in terms of both value for money and potential corruption.
- **Ethics.** Organisations may define the ethical framework that staff must operate under, including adherence to any national or international regulations or laws.

Governance and professional services

Among the aspects of professional services where it is particularly important that the governance systems are effective and appropriate is the matter of personal relationships. An organisation may not mind the chief financial officer having a round of golf to discuss the audit with a partner of the auditing firm, but where should the line be drawn? What if the round of golf involves a weekend at Gleneagles? Professional services firms are large users of corporate hospitality, and as is often said, "there is no such thing as a free lunch".

The big fear is that close relationships become corrupt ones. In the majority of cases, fraud involves someone inside a purchasing organisation and someone outside it. A common fraud arises when a supplier bills for more than was supplied, or for a higher specification than was delivered, with an "inside person" signing off the invoice or delivery records.

Military purchasing in the United States has had cases of vastly inflated prices being charged and authorised, perhaps caused by incompetence, but in some cases indistinguishable from corruption. Indeed, in October 2006, the US Department of Justice announced the formation of a National Procurement Fraud Task Force designed to promote the early detection, identification, prevention and prosecution of procurement fraud associated with the increase in contracting activity for national security and other government programmes. For example, the department announced in May 2009:

> A 23-count indictment unsealed today alleges that a civilian contractor paid more than $2.8m in bribes to a US army contracting official stationed at Camp Arifjan, an army base in Kuwait, and the official's wife, and that the three individuals committed services fraud and money-laundering offences in connection with the same conduct.

The risk of fraud in cases involving professional services – with someone signing off invoices for more days' consulting work than has been provided – is equally real; "professionals" do not always behave professionally.

Ethics should not need to be taught, but to ensure ethical behaviour it is good practice for organisations to state clearly what is allowable and what is not. Building relationships is important but it should be done circumspectly. Exploring markets properly to find the most appropriate suppliers and negotiate good deals can all be undercut by a relationship fuelled by hospitality and gifts. A further danger is that internal managers may have ambitions to move into professional services and may consider that awarding a contract to a firm they would like to work for will help their career prospects.

Compliance and sanctions: making it stick

The approach to dealing with serious breaches of purchasing policy, such as those described above, is clear-cut: action should be swift and uncompromising. Less serious breaches of policy are more difficult. Immediate dismissal is a reasonable response to fraudulent activity, but what action should be taken in the case of a manager who awards a consulting contract without involving the purchasing department, or without executing the defined process? If no real action is taken, there will be less incentive for managers to comply with policy. So best practice would suggest some action is advisable to encourage appropriate behaviour, perhaps an informal or formal warning.

Organisations that fire staff for serious breaches of purchasing policy will find that the breaches stop quickly, but few have the courage to do this. An approach used by a large US financial services firm fell short of such draconian action, but it still worked well. The penalty for the first breach of policy was a $100 "fine", which was taken out of the budget of the offender's department; for the second it was a $1,000 fine and a verbal warning; and for the third it was a $10,000 fine and a final warning. But as the chief purchasing officer says, "We never got past the second offence." The beauty of the scheme was that staff believed it would be followed. It was seen as firm but fair. And it made a difference that it had been introduced by a CPO whose ability to influence his peers and act as an effective internal champion for his department was of the highest order.

The importance of management information

To enable demand to be managed and purchasing people to engage with the market from an informed standpoint, management information about the historical use of professional services and (as far as possible) future demand is crucial.

Understanding how much has been spent, in which areas and with which suppliers will help in negotiation and improve management of future demand. Basic information might distinguish between spending on consultancy and on legal services. At the next level, understanding the type of consultancy contract or how the contingent (temporary) labour cost is calculated (the split between the basic rate for the job and the provider's margin), or being able to analyse day or hourly rates from different legal providers, will help purchasers manage demand, negotiate new contracts and manage existing providers.

This information will usually come from computer systems that track contracts and orders placed, and then monitor services and payments against those contracts. It is possible to obtain useful data in other ways, but large organisations will struggle to develop a full and accurate picture purely from paper-based systems.

Enterprise resource planning (ERP) systems form the backbone of many organisations' process management, including management of the purchasing process. Historically, their purchasing capability was often based on handling purchases of goods used in manufacturing processes, such as components, food ingredients and packaging. They were good at handling the situation where X units of commodity Y were purchased at a price of $Z per unit, to be delivered on a specified date.

But such systems often struggled to handle the purchase of services, particularly complex services. There may not be a "unit" price (in a risk-reward consulting contract, for instance), commodities are not clearly defined and the concept of a "delivery date" may be meaningless (an open-ended call-off contract for legal services, for example). This meant purchasers were unable to compare suppliers in a meaningful way, or track levels and patterns of demand and use. It could even be difficult to establish whether a contract recorded by the system was a professional services contract at all because of unclear categorisation.

In recent years ERP systems have improved, and new software providers have emerged with a much stronger focus on the purchasing of services. Their products enable more accurate recording of contracts and orders, and more detailed information to be obtained in spend areas such as contingent labour and consulting. Armed with better management information, purchasers can identify where spending is occurring in their organisation. This will allow them to manage demand better, put in place appropriate contracts and control expenditure through the life of the contract. (This sort of software can also help with "sourcing" and supplier selection – see Chapter 11.)

Among other things, Tim Ussher's experience at Virgin Media (see below) highlights the importance of demand management in making sure spending on professional services is under control and how this is an essential step on the path to getting better value from service providers.

Virgin Media

After a series of mergers and acquisitions, Virgin Media was launched in 2007. It is now involved in the supply of cable TV, broadband, telephone and related services to some 5m customers in the UK. Its procurement director, Tim Ussher, joined in 2007 when the purchasing function was still in its infancy.

Ussher's experience in developing "green-field" purchasing sites was essential: he had been the first chief procurement officer at BSkyB, part of Rupert Murdoch's media empire and a major satellite broadcaster in the UK. One of his strengths is an ability to develop stakeholder relationships within the organisation and to persuade senior colleagues of the value of a strong purchasing function and processes. That ability has been central to how he has approached purchasing of consulting services at Virgin Media. Ussher says:

> With almost £1 billion a year spent by us on third-party services, consulting is a major category in our portfolio, accounting for tens of millions a year. When

I arrived, it wasn't being managed by the purchasing team at all. In fact, everyone told me that there was no point even trying, that it was something that was firmly in the "too difficult" basket! And it is a sensitive area: we're talking about relationships between our suppliers and the most senior people in our organisation. At the same time, I was sure we could add some value if we did things properly and carefully.

Ussher was well aware that suppliers could use those relationships to go over his head and subvert whatever process he tried to put in place, a scenario he clearly needed to avoid. He therefore introduced a process that placed emphasis first on managing the internal users of consulting and second on convincing suppliers of the benefits of the purchasing process so they did not try to subvert it:

We worked out who our top 20 main suppliers were, then we told them – and our users – that we were going to improve the way we worked with them. We didn't start by announcing we were going to cut their fee rates. We argued that there would be benefits for them but that we expected something in return. We weren't threatening to drop any of them.

Ussher and his team developed a set of specific terms and conditions:

We wanted to be fair, so we spent a lot of time looking at suppliers' standard terms and conditions, but we also made it clear that we would ultimately develop and use our bespoke set.

The terms and conditions addressed areas of inconsistency and value, such as definitions of a working day and expenses policy. These, as Ussher points out, "are areas where value can easily leak away if they are not controlled".

The next stages in the process were based on dialogue, not form-filling. Meetings were held with all the top suppliers individually:

We showed them our Virgin video – we wanted to sell ourselves as a preferred customer. They could then respond formally to the tender, proposing the range of services they could offer with capped prices for the various levels of consultants. In some cases, several rounds of negotiation followed, but at every stage we invited internal stakeholders along to the meetings. Few actually took us up on the offer, but it helped reassure them that they had a say in things, it wasn't a process the purchasing team was imposing on them.

The result has been a significant improvement in value:

We expect to save around 10%, several millions at least; but, just as importantly, our stakeholders have supported the process and view this as a successful and helpful piece of purchasing work. We've since circulated a guide to the process which gives information about suppliers, rates and capabilities to our senior managers. In effect, we've ended up with a framework, but for all significant pieces of work, users still come through my team and we will run further competitive processes, or negotiate as we see fit to extract more value.

When asked what happens if someone wants to use a firm which is not on the list, Ussher's pragmatism comes to the fore:

I would never try to make a framework like this mandatory. There are times when our stakeholders have a good reason to use a different provider, and if that's the case, our job is to help them do that. However, we've made sure that it's easier for people to use the list than not – for instance, the terms and conditions are already in place for suppliers on the list – but, if a user wants to go outside it, we look at the justification on its merits. The chief financial officer signs off all major consulting spend, so I work with him to assess the need for the alternative supplier. If we do use someone new, and they perform well, we may take them into our framework. The framework itself runs for 18 months, which is a good balance between the effort involved and the need to refresh it.

Ussher likens his approach to procurement to a steel gauntlet in a velvet glove:

Taking internal stakeholders with you is critical, but you can still deliver real value and savings through effective procurement processes.

9 Category management

A "category" in purchasing terms is used to define a group of items, bought by an organisation, that share similar properties, and for most major organisations it is at category level that purchasing strategies are developed and purchasing activities planned.

Long established in the retail sector, category management involves breaking down the range of products sold into discrete groups of similar or related products, and then running each of these categories as a business in its own right, with its own set of financial targets and strategies. As the concept spread from retailing to other business sectors, organisations initially applied category management principles to the purchasing of "direct" materials, such as components, raw materials or packaging in the case of a manufacturing business. The concept was later applied to technical support goods such as services, and more recently, despite initial doubts among some that it would be helpful, to professional services.

Category management principles

Historically, much purchasing was reactive, driven by a direct require-ment from a budget holder within an organisation. Purchasing (if there was a specific function) responded to that requirement and placed an order or a contract with a supplier. Most purchasing people specialised to only a limited degree; many bought a wide range of items, varying week by week and month by month as requested by the budget holder. The adoption of category management through a focus on a group of products or services with similar characteristics has brought a more considered approach to how the goods or services are purchased. It offers the oppor-tunity for purchasing as a function and purchasing staff to:

- look at the organisation's requirements for the goods or services within a category ahead of the day-to-day operational needs;
- take into account the business needs (demand, specification, supplier service and quality), as well as the commercial needs;
- consider the total costs involved in a purchase, including (potentially) running costs, disposal and such things as sustainability and how the purchase might support wider societal goals.

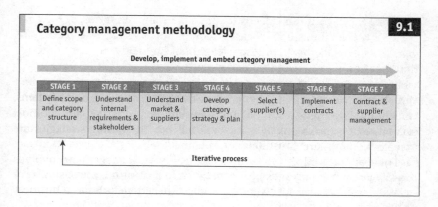

Category management methodology 9.1

Develop, implement and embed category management

STAGE 1	STAGE 2	STAGE 3	STAGE 4	STAGE 5	STAGE 6	STAGE 7
Define scope and category structure	Understand internal requirements & stakeholders	Understand market & suppliers	Develop category strategy & plan	Select supplier(s)	Implement contracts	Contract & supplier management

Iterative process

The implementation of category management is often best done as a project, with the requisite project processes and governance then following the organisation's purchasing policy and governance after implementation.

The many different category management methodologies include some common elements. Figure 9.1 illustrates a seven-stage approach. The first three stages define the work needed to understand the nature of the goods or services being bought. That understanding includes the outward-facing factors relating to the market – such as suppliers and the goods or services themselves – and the internal factors – what the organisation requires from the goods or services and the suppliers, and the interface with internal users. The fourth stage is the formation of the category strategy and plan, sometimes called a sourcing plan; this is the centrepiece of the process. The three subsequent stages see the plan delivered and the strategy implemented.

Stage 1: Define the scope and category structure
The first step is to determine the categories and subcategories, the logical groupings of expenditure, according to such factors as commonality of suppliers and common usage of the product or service.

In order to segment spend sensibly, a hierarchy of categories is helpful, the number of layers of which will depend on the size of the spend and the particular characteristics of the category. The top level may be defined as "master" categories, such as professional services, information technology, or packaging materials. At the second level the categories for professional services include management consulting, legal services or audit. In some large organisations, a third level under, say, management consulting might include strategic or purchasing consulting.

Overall, categorisation needs to strike a balance in terms of how far spend is broken into small blocks of requirements. A larger category may give more buying power, but may lead to an unwieldy category description that has little logic in the marketplace.

In drawing up a hierarchy of categories, the master category of professional services can be segmented into categories such as management consulting, legal services, audit services and so on. These can then be segmented into such subcategories as strategy, marketing and IT in the case of management consulting, or M&As, property and litigation in the case of legal services. Or categories might be divided into subcategories (or subcategories into sub-subcategories) by region – North America, Europe or Asia – or by individual countries in which the client firm does business or has plans to do business.

This segmentation and definition of categories is critical for professional services, which may be global and wide-ranging or local and specialised. Category overlap is also common. "Temporary labour", for example, may be defined as part of the professional services master category, but it could fit under a "human resources" master category, or a "recruitment services" category which could also sit under "human resources". There are similar examples in many professional services subcategories, and there is no right or wrong answer in terms of how an organisation segments and considers the spend areas; there is no standard or widely used structure for categorisation and most organisations segment based on their own spend profile and assessment of priority.

It may be sensible to consider the skills available within the purchasing organisation when categorising. For example, professional services involving property and construction may sit better in a "property" master category if the skills required to carry out this work successfully are already available within an existing property purchasing team.

However an organisation decides to segment, it is important that:

- all significant spending is picked up somewhere in the overall category mapping;
- duplication is avoided – approaching the same spend from different angles (because it falls within the remit of more than one manager) is inefficient and will confuse the market;
- links are in place across categories. If "temporary labour" ends up within "human resources", there should be a clear link with the "professional services" master category to make sure that knowledge of suppliers or processes is shared and that

governance is consistent across spend areas where appropriate. An organisation that makes it difficult for managers to engage consultants, while it is easy to take on temporary or contingent labour, will find that users exercise some creative budget management. "Consulting" spend will decline while "contingent labour" spend increases.

Stage 2: Understand internal requirements and stakeholders

Developing a strategy for the future has to be done in the light of the present. Category managers must be familiar with the current spend, the supplier situation and the internal demand for goods or services in terms of quantity, quality, specification and service requirements. The areas to be analysed include the following:

- Current expenditure by category and subcategory.
- The spending pattern and any relevant factors such as seasonality and regional differences.
- The likelihood of changes in spending.
- How goods or services that are currently purchased are used in the business, together with their importance and strategic value.
- The main users, specifiers or other influencers of the spend (for instance, staff in the IT department who may provide input to the services purchased) and their perception of the goods and services and the suppliers of them.
- Compliance with existing contracts.
- Current specifications and the likelihood of any changes in them over the next few years. Also the potential for changes to deliver greater value.
- Cost drivers, both internal (demand, specification) and external (market pressures, technology).

Outward-facing relationships should also be looked at, for example:

- How well regarded current suppliers are in the marketplace.
- How satisfactory the balance of power is with suppliers, and changes that would improve the relationship.

Stage 2 helps identify opportunities, risks and shortcomings with a view to determining what the category strategy needs to address.

Stage 3: Understand the market and suppliers

A good understanding of the requirement and the current position puts a category manager in a position to build up knowledge of the market, including the following:

Characteristics
- Size (including geographical data)
- Number of suppliers, market shares, concentration
- Historical development and future market growth
- Static or dynamic (in terms of new entrants, changes in market share or position)
- Impact of innovation or technology
- Power balances between suppliers and buyers

Suppliers, both those used and others who could be
- Past and present performance
- Size, financial strength, geographical coverage
- Business strategy, financial margins and cost structures
- Historical development and growth prospects
- Strengths and weaknesses
- Product or service offerings and competitive advantage

The market analysis must be driven by outputs from Stage 2 in terms of the organisation's requirements and how far they are being met. So, for example, if the internal review shows widespread dissatisfaction with current suppliers, an emphasis should be put on pinpointing potential new suppliers. Equally, if the internal analysis suggests a demand for consultants who can operate in a consistent manner globally, this is an obvious point of focus for Stage 3. The aim is to ensure appropriate focus and relevance, while retaining an open mind in terms of anything useful that the market analysis might reveal.

Stage 4: Develop category strategy and plan

This stage, which is in three parts, determines the strategies and plans that, if successful, drive better value and performance from professional services providers.

Formulate category options
It is at this stage that the category manager must draw together the research and analysis that have been carried out and determine how

the category is to be addressed. What is the organisation going to do to manage this category well? How will it award and manage contracts? How many suppliers and of what type are needed in each subcategory? How will competitive prices and appropriate service levels be obtained? However detailed and structured the category methodology used is, it cannot tell a manager what will work best. There are usually a number of sourcing approaches to consider, and they are not mutually exclusive, in which case various options should be developed for consideration, analysis and discussion.

Options that may help achieve better value in professional services categories include the following:

- **Leverage.** Can an organisation's buying power be used better? Can the supplier base be consolidated, using fewer suppliers in a particular category and negotiating better deals with them on the basis of more business – or the threat of less business? "We achieved reductions of 10–20% off rate card by putting in place a fairly basic consultancy preferred supplier list" was the message from a chief purchasing officer of a major communications firm. A sole supplier or a limited supply base should achieve better pricing, but at what cost in other terms? Less choice of supplier may mean less innovation, or suppliers without the required capability. Few professional services providers can cover every aspect of the market; and internal stakeholders are likely to lack enthusiasm for actions that reduce the choice of supplier.
- **Competition/supply market activity.** Are there market opportunities that can drive benefits? For instance, new suppliers with a lower cost base may be found in other countries, or cheaper local legal firms may be useful for some transactions instead of larger firms. The possibility that business may be diverted to these cheaper suppliers may encourage current suppliers to increase efficiency or reduce prices.
- **Demand management.** Is it possible to save money simply by spending less? Can policies be introduced to tighten the approval process for engaging consultants, or can the percentage of expenditure going to preferred suppliers be increased?
- **Specification management.** Are the most appropriate specifications being used? Are top firms being used when less pricy alternatives can do the job just as well? Are unnecessary costs being incurred because the specification is unclear or too vague?

- **Strategic partnering.** Is a strategic relationship with a supplier (see Chapter 19) worth investigating? This may not bring conventional purchasing savings but could add value in the wider organisational sense, perhaps through entering a partnership with that supplier to develop a new business together in another country.
- **Process change.** Are transactional processes as efficient as possible? Can invoicing be consolidated into one electronic monthly invoice rather than processing 200 invoices a month from the same firm?
- **Outsourcing (and insourcing) opportunities.** Can any business process be outsourced? For instance, an organisation may have an internal legal function and engage external lawyers on a regular basis. Other options might be to outsource all legal advice or to insource by taking on more internal legal staff and reducing external expenditure on legal advice. The benefits of outsourcing or increased insourcing may far outweigh those achieved through leverage.

Choose the strategy
When the options have been arrived at, the factors to consider include the following:

- How much will the option cost to implement?
- How easy will it be to achieve?
- What are the likely effects on the business?
- What are the risks or unknown factors and how quantifiable are they, that is, what is the likelihood of success?
- What will the benefits be and are they sustainable?
- How will stakeholders perceive the preferred strategy and how will you manage them?

Options analysis can be used to determine the potential benefits, assessed against the risks and uncertainties. The category options that appear to have the best likely outcomes and benefits can then be chosen.

Draw up the category strategy and plan
This may be a two-stage process. Many organisations produce a category strategy document that goes through some sort of approval process at a senior level and that usually but not always includes details of

the implementation plan; it is hard to approve a strategy without any knowledge of the likely cost, resource implication or timescale needed to implement it. The inclusion of a summary or high-level implementation plan as part of the strategy document ensures that a view can be taken of the cost/benefit equation, without too much time being wasted on detailed project planning if the strategy is rejected or changed significantly.

A category strategy and plan document can be structured as follows:

- Objectives and purpose
- Identification of stakeholders (multi-functional approach)
- Spend identification
- Description of cost drivers
- Market and supplier analysis and research
- Sourcing approach
- Process issues
- Quantification of benefits (including options analysis where appropriate)
- Action plan and responsibility (see below for more detail)
- Summary and conclusions

The outline plan should cover the following topics, if only at a high level:

- What activities are necessary to deliver the strategy?
- What are the milestones and deliverables?
- Who will be responsible for delivery?
- What resources (human, physical, financial) are needed to achieve the plan?
- What governance and reporting arrangements are necessary?
- What are the risks and how will they be addressed?
- What benefits will be delivered (cash and non-cash) and what is the estimated cost of implementing the plan (cost/benefit analysis)?

A more detailed plan can then be developed once the strategy is approved. The approval process should be clearly defined, and so constructed to make sure that all the important internal stakeholders support what is approved. For example, if 90% of the current legal services providers are to be dispensed with, the internal director responsible for legal services must be content.

Stage 5: Select suppliers

The category strategy and plan defines the subsequent implementation phases. These are covered more fully in Parts 4, 5 and 6 of this book, which look at supplier selection processes and contract and supplier management.

The selection of suppliers may involve a competitive process that leads to the appointment of a single supplier or many suppliers, or a framework of some sort. Alternatively, the supplier selection process may be non-competitive, or there may be no supplier to select because the strategy is to insource.

Stage 6: Implement contracts

Implementation may be straightforward with contractual arrangements with current suppliers remaining much the same. If new suppliers are introduced, particularly if they replace current suppliers, transition and implementation can be complex and may require careful planning.

Stage 7: Contract and supplier management

The activities that take place after contracts are in place are in many cases more critical to overall success than the pre-contract activities (see Chapters 18 and 19). These activities may include:

- contract monitoring and management;
- supplier relationship management;
- benchmarking and market testing;
- maintenance of market awareness and understanding.

Generally, a category plan will contain an outline of how the contracts and suppliers are to be managed. It may include key performance indicators or other metrics and processes, responsibilities for contract management activity and some discussion of supplier management. It generally will not contain the details of specific contractual performance measures or strategic matters to do with supplier relationships; these will be developed as part of a specific contracting proposal or business case.

Continuing category management

Following implementation, the category manager needs to reappraise the stages involved in the process to make sure that aspects such as market research and awareness are kept up to date.

Furthermore, the category strategy should be reviewed according to a timeframe that aligns with the contracting strategy. If the strategy is three-year framework contracts for professional services providers, the strategy should be reviewed around two years into that period, in good time to introduce any desirable changes in the next contractual round. However, the category manager, as well as being engaged in contract and supplier management activity, should be keeping a close eye on internal requirements and market developments. If circumstances change, appropriate action, where possible, can be taken before the end of current contracts.

In developing and improving a category management approach it is important to be alert to the opportunities there may be for getting additional value through the use of suppliers that work across a number of different categories (see Chapter 19 on supplier relationship management).

Ultimately, as Malcolm Harrison of Nestlé highlights below, successful category management comes down to people as much as process – notably the capability of category managers and the way in which the purchasing department engages with internal stakeholders and the skills they have or develop through training.

Nestlé

Malcolm Harrison's career stretched from being the rabbit meat buyer for Pedigree Petfoods to top purchasing jobs in global companies selling chocolate, coffee and beer.

Since 2006 he has been the global chief purchasing officer for Nestlé, with functional responsibility for over 1,000 purchasing staff and a central team of around 50. Nestlé is the biggest food company in the world and one of the 30 biggest companies of any type. Its brands include Nescafé, the biggest coffee brand in the world, Kit Kat, Shreddies, Maggi, Carnation, Felix and Buxton Water. It has an annual turnover of roughly $110 billion, employs around 280,000 staff and runs 450 factories in over 80 countries. More than half of its turnover is spent on third-party suppliers in areas ranging from categories where Nestlé is the largest purchaser in the world, for example milk powders, where over 500,000 tonnes a year are purchased, to indirect categories such as travel, professional services and fleet. Nestlé operates a matrix structure, with geographical organisation (such as the UK) and strategic business units (such as confectionery). Geographical decentralisation means that central functions such as procurement work through persuasion and influence by demonstrating value, rather than through compulsion.

Harrison emphasises that category management cannot work without influencing and engaging senior stakeholders, and that staff capability is about understanding strategic linkages to the business as much as technical procurement skills. His 25 years of top-level experience have taught him that successful purchasing requires a focus on three areas: staff capability, purchasing processes and stakeholder management. What is especially interesting is how he sees the priorities:

Category management success is at least as much about staff capability and stakeholder management as it is about the core category management process.

In recent years, Nestlé has implemented a common category management approach. It is a seven-step process which includes steps such as demand and specification management, market and supplier analysis and development of sourcing strategies, with a central team managing processes, systems and capability across the functional group, as well as directly managing a small number of global categories. These global categories are chosen for their overall importance to Nestlé (such as skimmed milk powder and coffee) and because there are limited local supply markets; no coffee beans are grown in European countries, for example.

Outside the centrally led global commodities, category management is carried out across a wide range of business units and countries, so developing skills is essential to the success of the category process at local level and more widely. Harrison says:

Leveraging skills and expertise is more important than aggregating pure scale or volume: staff capability is a key constraint on the speed of implementation of the programme. We've therefore put a lot of effort into developing the capability of Nestlé staff to execute the process. To implement across the whole business and all 1000+ procurement staff, we launched a global "train the trainer" programme: a few dozen people went through this process, and then trained all staff in the individual countries and business units – with the local training often done in the native language of the buyers.

Procurement people need to combine two sets of capabilities. First, they must have deep category knowledge: "they really have to understand the levers for their category", as Harrison puts it. This means being aware of the different potential approaches for categories and choosing the most appropriate in each case. In some cases, Nestlé will use competitive bidding; in others – for instance, where it is a major player in that category – a more subtle approach may be needed. Ensuring supply may be the prime objective of the procurement activity, but Harrison believes that professional services categories are among the most complex:

In some professional service areas, there are few real global players so we will work at regional or national level. But there is a skill in identifying subcategories and different approaches. For instance, in the market research area, we have worked to identify elements that we might look at more globally and where we may be able to use our leverage and get more value. In other aspects of market research, the expertise we need is local, so we will look to set up frameworks and preferred supplier deals at that national level. There is no one-size-fits-all solution.

The second set covers broader procurement skills – technical skills (such as negotiation and supplier analysis) and also communication and change management capability, and the ability to deal with a wide range of stakeholders successfully:

Eventually, we may need better procurement staff, rather than more procurement staff, as more collaboration leads to fewer contracts which have to be managed far more professionally. But the task of considering key categories on a global scale will need considerable skill and change leadership; it is wrong to assume that good local level category managers will always be able to step up from that level, although I'm sure many of our people will make the step.

In terms of managing senior stakeholders, the country or strategic business unit must be ready for collaboration, which is often carried out incrementally. If units within a country are not working together well, or indeed procurement people are not involved in a specific spending category at a local level, there is no point trying to engage them in global initiatives. So gaining agreement to a national framework for legal services will be pursued before there is an attempt to bring a country into a global agreement.

Harrison expands on this theme:

We must have a "pull" from businesses rather than relying on a "push" from procurement. Historically, procurement relied on push to try to achieve collaborative outcomes. Without prior commitment from the businesses to centrally negotiated activity, local deals would be done which were often better than "group deals", which undermined the credibility of the central procurement function. So we start the stakeholder engagement process at an early stage in considering any spend category. Beyond this, there must be governance and structure to collaborative procurement activity. Where a category is being considered across geographies, we involve senior business people from the beginning. Their commitment makes it harder for local procurement staff to resist central initiatives.

This enables a central procurement department to exert governance based on this standard process. If a local business has followed the standard category management process and decides not to collaborate, the centre is unlikely to oppose that decision. But if the standard process was not followed, Harrison and the central team will raise this with the local senior procurement or business managers.

Despite good progress in the past couple of years, Harrison assesses that Nestlé is still only 20% through its journey towards optimal category management, including the professional service areas, and that it will take 5–10 years to get close to that point. "There are no magic bullets," he concludes, "just a lot of effort and skill, systematically and consistently applied."

10 Frameworks and approved suppliers

The majority of large organisations use frameworks or similar approaches – such as preferred supplier lists (PSLs) and approved suppliers or vendors – as part of their category management strategies for purchasing professional services, although some use them better than others. The terminology may differ, but all these approaches share common characteristics, and almost all the senior purchasing executives interviewed for this book make extensive use of them.

The underlying principle is that a limited number of suppliers are chosen in advance of a specific purchasing requirement arising within a category. But the list of suppliers may be used in different ways. It may meet all of the requirements in that category or just some of them; it may be formal with detailed terms and conditions in place or merely an informal list of useful potential providers.

For instance, an organisation may draw up a list of ten legal firms to provide all the legal services needed for the next three years. The list may then be referred to as a framework or a preferred supplier list.

This approach of developing frameworks or similar mechanisms is generally used for either or both of the following:

- To simplify the appointment of a professional services provider when the need for one arises.
- To negotiate better terms with suppliers, for whom the incentive is the potential benefit of becoming part of a pre-approved or preferred group.

Terms and their meanings

- **An approved supplier** has met an organisation's selection criteria. However, "approval" may carry no commitment to future business, although it should give the category-approved supplier some preference over a non-approved supplier.
- **A preferred supplier** will be given some element of preference, such as some guarantee or estimate of volume in terms of likely spend, over a non-preferred supplier. But even where there is a preferred supplier list (PSL), other suppliers may be used depending on the buyer's chosen approach.

- **A framework** comprises a number of suppliers who have some sort of preferred status. Some overarching general contractual terms and conditions may be agreed between buyers and suppliers, but generally no contract is formed until a buyer places an order with a supplier – usually termed a call-off. This is because the framework does not provide all the required criteria for a contract, which in most countries include offer, acceptance and consideration or payment. The framework may involve any number of suppliers, although if there is only one it may be termed a "call-off contract/agreement" or a "blanket contract" rather than a framework. As in the case of preferred suppliers, a framework may not guarantee future contracts.

Using frameworks and preferred supplier lists

When developing a framework or a preferred supplier list, the following should be considered:

- **Mandation.** How strong is the preference for the suppliers listed? Should users of professional services be able to buy from suppliers who are not on the list?
- **Flexibility.** Is the list fixed for a significant period of time (three or four years in the case of public-sector frameworks is usual), or is it regularly renewed with the opportunity for new suppliers to be listed? Can users suggest new suppliers to join the list? This may make the list more acceptable to users, but it will reduce the value suppliers will offer to be part of it.
- **Contractualisation.** How much of the final contract between the parties is agreed when the framework or PSL is first set up, the rest being left to the point of contract formation (call-off or similar)?

At one extreme, a framework or preferred supplier list may be no more than a guide to some potentially useful firms that have been through a quick approval process and may be able to fulfil specific needs as they arise, and it may give suppliers no guarantee that they will be used. There may also be no contractual terms agreed in advance. At the other extreme, there could be a short list of suppliers who are the only ones to be used in a particular category. A large proportion of the final terms and conditions of the contract could already be in place, including pricing, and the award of a specific piece of work or call-off is then little more than a confirmation of what the work is and when it is to be done by.

Most organisations use preferred supplier lists or frameworks to some extent in the purchasing of professional services. Table 10.1 summarises the advantages and disadvantages.

Table 10.1 **Designing frameworks and preferred supplier lists: pros and cons**

	Pros	Cons
Mandation: we must follow the purchasing rules	Increases purchasing department's influence Reduces maverick spending Puts pressure on purchasing department to perform	Potential hostility from stakeholders Poor purchasing will lead to inappropriate suppliers being used
Flexibility: we do not regularly review and refresh the list	Develops closer supplier relationships Helps guarantee some volume to suppliers Convenience: no need to go to market for each assignment	Supplier complacency, loss of flexibility and competitiveness Misses out on new entrants to market Lowest common denominator supplier choice
Contractualisation: we will use these pre-agreed terms and conditions	Guarantees sensible, standard terms and conditions Protects less competent users Ability to negotiate competitive rates Faster supplier engagement (as terms and conditions already in place)	Inflexible; terms and conditions may not be suitable in every case Vulnerable to supplier manipulation, eg on grading and rates Unlikely to achieve best rates without competition and commitment

Advantages of frameworks and preferred supplier lists

◪ **Time saving and faster purchasing.** Having a list of approved suppliers, with some contract terms already negotiated, saves time and is well suited to the public sector. Private-sector firms with urgent requirements are free to act in ways they deem necessary. Public-sector bodies are generally more constrained and, therefore, when a requirement is urgent, it can be useful to have a pre-selected framework, thus avoiding the need to go through a full tendering process.

- **Assure quality.** A pre-selection process can help to ensure that the suppliers eventually used are suitable and likely to provide the right quality service.
- **Establish terms and conditions.** A framework or preferred supplier list provides a level of contractual security. Having appropriate terms and conditions agreed in advance in theory reduces risk – even if in practice this cannot ensure compliance.
- **Control.** Directing internal users and budget holders towards agreed suppliers ensures a level of control and governance over costs as well as factors mentioned above such as quality and risk management.
- **Value for money.** Most organisations will hope to achieve some value advantage through a framework or preferred supplier list. To get a place on the list a preferred supplier will have been judged to offer the purchasing organisation a benefit not available from a non-listed supplier. That may be related to quality, price, the acceptance of more onerous contractual terms, and so on. But suppliers need confidence that being on the list will be beneficial; otherwise they are unlikely to offer anything significant in return.
- **Opportunity for relationship development.** The existence of preferred suppliers provides both the buying organisation and the suppliers the incentive and opportunity to develop stronger relationships (see Chapter 19).
- **Legislative compliance.** Linked to the speed advantage, particularly in the public sector, is the comfort that legally compliant frameworks can be used in the knowledge that there is no danger of breaking procurement regulations.

Disadvantages of frameworks and preferred supplier lists

Loss of flexibility and the advantages of a competitive environment

Preferred supplier lists can result in an organisation becoming locked into using particular suppliers, which can lead to them becoming complacent and taking the business for granted. Generally, reducing competition does not lead to better value or performance.

Missing out on innovation and new market entrants

Preferred supplier lists, or frameworks, are particularly effective where requirements do not change rapidly or dramatically. A breadmaker's list of approved flour suppliers guarantees both an acceptable standard of quality and adequate supplies. The purchaser can then keep suppliers on their competitive toes through a system of regular bidding. The specification for flour remains more or less constant, and there are few new entrants into the market. Buying advertising is very different from buying flour. Much good work is done by relatively young agencies and it is likely that a preferred supplier list drawn up some years ago would not contain the range of firms that a marketing team would want to use. Being locked into a preferred supplier list with no scope for new entrants could exclude suppliers who would provide a significant competitive advantage.

Different types of professional services show different characteristics in this sense. Drawing up a preferred supplier list of global audit firms is not difficult; there are probably only four serious candidates (and have been for some years), and change in the market is slow. A global organisation that is a large buyer of such services may well be attracted to a framework or preferred supplier list because it avoids having to renegotiate terms country by country for each supplier. But in a more dynamic market the position is different. Suppose the buying organisation wants top-notch, "blue-sky" thinking, board-level strategic advice. This year, the person everyone wants is X. Next year, it will be someone else who is hot. Putting together a preferred supplier list of blue-sky thinkers would have little point beyond the short term and would do nothing in terms of helping to negotiate better value for money.

"Lowest common denominator" limitations

Some consulting or legal firms offer a wide range of services; others are specialist. The easiest thing for a purchasing manager to do is to set up a preferred supplier list with, for instance, well-known multidisciplinary consulting firms, or the "magic circle" London or New York law firms. Such firms may accept virtually any assignment that is put to them, but they may not always offer the best value for money compared with a niche player with smaller overheads; they may not be the most innovative or nimble; and they may not have the depth of specialist competence that a more focused firm has. Internal users of professional services are often closer to the market than the purchasing department, and know which firms offer the benefits they want as managers or budget holders. They will not be impressed if told such firms are "not on our preferred supplier list".

Commercial ...

In most markets, buyers will not be able to obtain the best prices until they have a real order to place and real money to spend. Professional services firms rarely offer their best rates on the basis of just being part of a framework or preferred supplier list. The best deal will be done when there is a deal to be done, and buyers should be wary of accepting framework pricing as it may not be sufficiently competitive.

... and contractual issues

Similarly, agreeing some terms and conditions in advance may be sensible but not at the cost of forsaking the leverage available when negotiating a firm deal. Framework terms and conditions should never be so tightly defined that they stop the buying organisation achieving what it wants contractually (and what is achievable through negotiation) for an assignment.

Not a panacea

Lee Sach, founding partner of New York and London-based Mosaic Financial Markets, a niche consulting firm specialising in the financial services sector, observes:

> The big banks and an increasing number of mid-sized ones
> have implemented significant changes to their procurement and
> vendor management processes over the last ten years.

One of the most important changes he has seen has been the involvement of senior managers in driving these processes:

> Executive management in the banks have used procurement
> functions as a way to curtail consulting spending they perceive
> to be "out of control". The greater involvement of procurement
> appears to be aimed not just at improving the purchasing power
> of the banks but also reducing the absolute level of spend on
> consultants made by individual buyers within the banks. As
> a result, the process is often designed to make it harder to get
> consulting spend approved and signed off.

But the main issue for Sach and his colleagues has been the growing number of preferred supplier lists (PSLs):

> One bank has recently upgraded its procurement approach to
> rationalise the many hundreds of service providers who had
> proliferated over the years to a more manageable number. This
> bank has now put in place a PSL of tens of suppliers; this not

only includes many of the big players, but also gives room for specialist firms like ours. Another bank maintains a PSL with a select handful of major vendors, with a back-up list of approved niche suppliers who are only typically invited to bid for work the larger suppliers aren't able to execute, making it especially hard for specialists to compete.

Size is not the only barrier Sach faces:

Banks typically seem to divide their professional services vendors into three categories: offshore companies; management or IT consulting firms; and staff support or "augmentation" firms, supplying interim managers and contractors. Our business is a hybrid offering that covers both the second and third types, but clients typically put us in the second category, with commodity "body-shops" fiercely competing in the third. This restricts our ability to provide senior-level advisory services based upon a single industry consultant working as part of client teams to help shape or steer complex projects early on in the project life cycle. Client buyers can get very frustrated: they often have to justify using specialist industry firms and see no advantage in trying to use big firms on the PSL for these specialist needs.

Increasingly, clients are outsourcing pieces of the vendor management process to third parties, which makes it harder still for us as we end up dealing with people who are very removed from the end-users' business.

The bottom line for us is that the typical sales cycle has lengthened considerably and that we spend significantly more time managing the sales process than we did before. That said, a robust procurement process brings benefits to vendors too, including better visibility of our clients' pipelines of prospective consulting work, and raises the barriers to entry for firms competing against us where we're on the PSL.

He sums up his experience:

As a new business, we've focused our efforts on building a portfolio of client PSLs by trying to win engagements with buyers prepared to sponsor us on to their PSL. Fortunately, we've been extremely lucky to have the support of some strong relationships.

While the banks doubtless needed to improve and tighten their procurement functions, it feels like it's now much harder to do business with them, particularly as a small player, and that our overall costs have escalated sharply. Ultimately, the client has to pay for these costs one way or another, and it may mean clients won't get the same quality of service they were used to in the past.

How to use frameworks

Frameworks and preferred supplier lists do not always guarantee value for money, and they may in some cases enshrine day rates that, unless renegotiated, are not competitive. They also discourage users from developing often more appropriate payment mechanisms (such as fixed price or risk share), or using more innovative and specialist firms. The existence of a framework, especially one with a top-tier firm, makes it easy internally to stick to the framework day rates, which are generally perceived to be set in stone.

Despite their drawbacks, frameworks and preferred supplier lists can be useful for buying professional services category provided three conditions are met:

- A sufficient spend to justify the effort of all those involved in setting up the framework.
- A spread of usage across the framework; if only one supplier is ever used, it is a waste of time developing a preferred supplier list.
- Organisational commitment to using the framework. Without that, the odds are that the framework will be ignored and prove to have been a pointless exercise. The purchasing team at an international financial services firm set up a complex framework only to find a year later that some 90% of spending in that category was still going to non-framework suppliers.

Assuming these conditions are fulfilled, there are a number of considerations that must be addressed to ensure appropriate frameworks are put in place and then managed in a manner that delivers what internal users require. These include the following:

- **Frameworks must deliver value for money.** Many simply do not. The best price is usually obtained if there is a commitment to spend and volume. Negotiating is tougher without a guarantee of a certain amount of work in the future.

◪ **Seek to make some commitment to volume or spend** where possible to obtain competitive rates from suppliers. Negotiating is tougher without a guarantee of a certain amount of work in the future.

◪ **Avoid getting locked into pricing** unless volume can be fully guaranteed up front. By all means agree standard terms and conditions, but keep some flexibility to negotiate further once actual business is on offer to suppliers. Kristine Moore at Shell (see page 53) puts considerable effort into benchmarking prices and regularly refreshing frameworks.

◪ **Make use of further competition.** Competition between firms on the preferred supplier list, or even involving "outsiders", is often the way to extract the best possible value from the preferred suppliers. But if a full competition is run for every requirement, there is little point in setting up the list in the first place, so a balance needs to be struck here.

◪ **Segment the framework or preferred supplier list** according to the range of services required and the level of spend, taking into account the likely use of the framework. Consulting can be segmented into strategic, multidisciplinary or specialist (HR, procurement, and so on) advice. Legal services can be segmented into the type of legal issue, country or region, or complexity of the case, or a combination of these.

◪ **Retain flexibility** in the ability to remove or add suppliers as and when it is desired to do so. A list should not be cast in concrete for several years. Markets change and useful new providers emerge. Flexibility is harder to ensure in the public sector but can be addressed by, for example, putting in place a set of frameworks with overlapping content and staggered termination dates.

Frameworks and supplier management

Once a framework or preferred supplier list is in place, it gives the opportunity to develop supplier relationships beyond day-to-day contract management. But just because a supplier is on a preferred supplier list does not mean it has strategic value. In the case of a breadmaker, the flour suppliers on its framework are unlikely to have strategic value unless the market is prone to supply problems. So each supplier should be assessed as described in Chapter 19 to determine how it is best managed, and whether it is worth applying supplier management processes.

There is a danger that suppliers who are included in a framework or preferred supplier list expect special treatment and that if they do not receive any, it sours the relationship. Similarly, if suppliers are not given any further business (for whatever reason) once they are listed, their motivation and the relationship are likely to deteriorate. So it is important to manage expectations and make it clear from the earliest stages of developing the framework the position suppliers are in, and to provide feedback on performance and how the framework is being used.

At the BBC (see below) extensive use is made of framework agreements and they have been set up with care to allow use of "second-tier" consulting firms that offer specialist expertise or greater value for money. Also stressed to suppliers on the frameworks is the BBC's requirement that skills are transferred and residual value created when a supplier is selected to work on a project.

The British Broadcasting Corporation

The BBC may be universally familiar but it is an unusual organisation in many respects. It is the largest broadcasting corporation in the world, funded by licence fees, rather than advertising, to provide services including national television channels and regional programmes, national and local radio stations, and an extensive website, bbc.co.uk. Government funding in addition to the licence fee supports the BBC World Service broadcasts to the world, providing news and information in 32 languages. On top of this, there is BBC Worldwide, the commercial arm, which operates businesses including selling programmes around the world and publishing books, DVDs and merchandise. Its profits are returned to the BBC for investment in new programming and services.

This mixture of public and commercial funding means that, on the one hand, the BBC is bound by government purchasing regulations: it has to advertise most major purchasing requirements in the *Official Journal of the European Union* (*OJEU*), issue a formal invitation to tender and go through a full procurement process. On the other hand, the BBC operates in a highly competitive environment, and the time involved in appointing a supplier via the *OJEU* process might compromise its ability to maintain a competitive advantage. This is one reason the BBC makes extensive use of framework agreements to meet its supply needs in the professional services area.

Jim Hemmington, head of strategic contracts at the BBC, says:

The development of iPlayer is a good example. We needed specialist expertise, and in such circumstances, where speed and confidentiality would be critical, a "normal" organisation would just quickly appoint the best supplier for the job and begin work. In our case, unless we used a supplier from our existing frameworks, we would have been forced to compromise our competitive position by making a very public OJEU announcement and to lose valuable time in the procurement process around the selection of a supplier.

Having the right mix of suppliers appointed to its framework agreements is therefore critical for the BBC:

It's the reason why, for an organisation with tight controls on expenditure on professional services, we still have a relatively large supplier base. We segment our requirements and set up frameworks with multiple suppliers across a number of different consulting subcategories.

Hemmington's purchasing strategy for consultancy has three constraints: managing demand and effective commissioning; committing the right internal resources to assignments; making sure that residual value is extracted from the assignment wherever possible. He says:

As a purchasing group, we have a particularly strong role to play when it comes to managing and challenging demand. Having frameworks in place doesn't mean stakeholders can just go and engage consultants. My team will make sure that stakeholders define their requirements and the expected deliverables from an assignment as clearly as possible, and ensure the best supplier is chosen for the task in hand. Committing the right internal resources is something we have to rely on our customers [internal managers] to think about: we have to be an intelligent client and understand that the success of an assignment depends as much on what we do as what the supplier does.

Rather than bringing in professional advisers and leaving them alone to do their job, the BBC plays an active role, assigning internal staff to a project to monitor, assess and make changes where necessary.

But it is the third strand – extracting residual value – which has been the cornerstone of the BBC's professional services purchasing strategy over recent years. As with many other public-sector bodies, skills transfer is crucial. As Hemmington puts it:

The value an adviser adds should not end with their final report. We have to be willing to enter into risk-reward agreements with consulting suppliers and to think innovatively about how such partnerships might be structured – while recognising that money is not the only measure of value – to ensure that skills are transferred and that practical solutions, not just reports, are delivered.

How does this work in practice? Any BBC stakeholder wishing to commission a consultant starts by creating a brief and sending it to Hemmington's team. The team works with the user to define the business criteria and, where appropriate, determine which framework will meet the need. Extensive information on suppliers is available on the BBC's purchasing intranet. At the same time, the user submits a business case, indicating the expected benefits and likely costs, and requests budgetary approval. When it is approved, Hemmington's team moves forward with the commissioning process. This may include running a competition between framework suppliers (which may take the form of a reverse auction), and looking at appropriate pricing structures (see Chapter 13).

Despite the focus on value, the extent to which the BBC tries to build collaborative relationships with its suppliers, and share both risks and rewards with them, is what sets its approach to purchasing professional services apart. Even at the pre-qualification stage of the purchasing process (see Chapter 11), willingness to engage in a collaborative approach, including the transfer of skills during an assignment, is an evaluation criterion. Hemmington says:

> Risk-reward works in relation to consulting projects if the assignment has clear deliverables and you have a team to work in parallel with the consultants. You have to start by asking what you're trying to achieve, as well as the dependencies across the organisation as a whole. If you can articulate and measure these, risk-reward will be an appropriate and effective tool.

The risk-reward approach is a recent step the BBC has taken to make sure it gets good value from consultants. The result has been greater use of "second-tier" consulting firms and a greater focus on the delivery of benefits. Hemmington points out:

> The archetypal consulting process has three phases: scoping, recommendations and delivery. We're turning the discussions round so that we talk about the deliverables first, what we want to achieve from a business point of view. Having defined that value, we're in a better position to be clear about what we want to achieve from consulting firms.

Sometimes this takes the form of actual savings, but there are non-financial objectives as well. For example, there has been an increased emphasis on skills transfer, thus ensuring that the BBC learns from consultants rather than becomes dependent on them. Hemmington says:

> We've changed the nature of the dialogue we have when we commission

a consulting project to focus on the skills we want to acquire and the responsibilities each side has in the process.

The incentives offered to a consulting firm may also be non-financial. Although the BBC may link fees to performance, it is willing to act as a reference site (a project that the supplier can use as a positive example to impress other potential clients) or to allow a consulting firm to use the intellectual capital created in a specific assignment for other clients.

According to Hemmington, there are two critical factors in making a risk-reward approach work with consultants:

The first is ensuring you have agreement from the finance department on the numbers. At the BBC, all consulting projects have to be approved by the finance director, and the first things she's going to ask is what the savings are and what value will be created for our organisation. The second is to be absolutely sure how those benefits or savings are going to be delivered. It's not enough for the consultants just to make recommendations or write reports.

PART 4

CHOOSING THE RIGHT SUPPLIER

Particularly where professional services are concerned, all purchasing activities converge on one point: choosing the right supplier. The supplier determines the product, not the product the supplier.

This section covers the main stages of the selection process, from initial surveys of the professional services market, through drawing up a shortlist and inviting firms to submit proposals, to final selection. However, success does not depend solely on having the right process and following it. Also important is the selection of the criteria against which a professional services firm will be judged: its record and its ability to articulate what its services will be in a particular set of circumstances; the quality and abilities of the individual advisers put forward; and, finally, whether all this represents value for money.

11 The selection process

Selecting a supplier is at the heart of the purchasing task. It is the supplier who ultimately determines the success or failure of the process and choosing the "best" supplier is fundamental. Nothing is worse for the reputation of a purchasing department than the failure of a chosen supplier to perform.

Yet purchasing people sometimes forget this and become obsessed by the process. A high-profile contract failure in the UK education sector was investigated and the "procurement process was sound", according to the learned team that reviewed it. It was possible to see what this meant: the process was legal, thorough and fair. Yet a supplier was chosen that failed to deliver the operational requirements on time.

Competition is a crucial element in successful purchasing in general. A lack of competition leads to monopolistic-type behaviour and to complacency among suppliers, corruption and waste.

That lack of competition increases purchasing costs has been picked up at the highest level. The Presidential Memorandum on Government Contracting, issued by President Obama in March 2009, places particular emphasis on the need for competitive processes in US government purchasing. It states:

> Reports by agency Inspectors General, the Government Accountability Office (GAO), and other independent reviewing bodies have shown that non-competitive and cost-reimbursement contracts have been misused, resulting in wasted taxpayer resources, poor contractor performance, and inadequate accountability for results. When awarding government contracts, the federal government must strive for an open and competitive process.

Competition may not always be the best route. An assignment may have a level of confidentiality or urgency that makes open competition impossible; or it may be a follow-on to previous work that strongly suggests the same provider would be the best option. But a competitive process allows the purchaser to test the market and see which providers have real capability; it may lead to alternative methods being proposed for the work that the purchaser may not have considered; and it is likely to lead to more thoughtful and imaginative proposals and better value for money.

Basic principles

The three underlying principles to selecting suppliers are:

- Can they provide what we need – do they have the capability and capacity?
- Will they be good to work with – in terms of soundness, cultural compatibility and relationship potential?
- Are they offering the best solution to satisfying the requirement – in terms of value for money?

Whether the process is a formal, multi-stage one, which could take a year or more in extreme cases, or a short, sharp selection based on a quick proposal and a chat with a couple of potential suppliers, these principles remain the same.

Formal tenders or direct negotiation

There will be times when a formal selection process or "tendering" may not be necessary or advisable. If the assignment is small, time is short, or a framework or preferred supplier list (see Chapter 10) is in place, it may not be appropriate. But there are many times when a formal, tendering type process will be suitable, and some when it will be obligatory, as is usually the case for public-sector purchasing of professional services.

If you do not use a structured process, on what basis do you select a supplier? Pure guesswork, luck or subjective "feel" can hardly be relied upon to come up trumps. Without a process, how do you justify your decisions internally and to outside suppliers? Suppliers will quickly stop bidding for work if they think the selection process is unfair or random. Furthermore, if the process is not structured and transparent, what is to stop it becoming subject to favouritism or even corrupt?

Tendering process

As Figure 11.1 illustrates, the supplier selection process has four stages.

Stage 1: Market engagement and advertising

For large or sensitive assignments, or those where the market is ill-defined or limited, some engagement with the market before the formal process

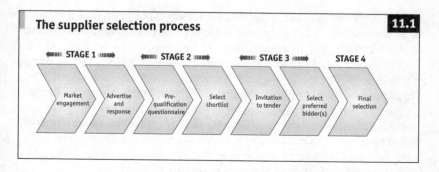

The supplier selection process | **11.1**

⬅▪▪▪ STAGE 1 ▪▪▪➡ ⬅▪▪▪ STAGE 2 ▪▪▪➡ ⬅▪▪▪ STAGE 3 ▪▪▪➡ STAGE 4

Market engagement | Advertise and response | Pre-qualification questionnaire | Select shortlist | Invitation to tender | Select preferred bidder(s) | Final selection

starts is often useful, and may even be essential, to stimulate interest. Engagement can be triggered by advertising or publicising the forthcoming opportunity, direct contact with known suppliers (although this must be handled carefully in the public sector and may not be allowed in some countries), or the use of trade press, known contacts, conferences or special events. The aim is to prepare the market so that interested and capable providers are ready to respond when the formal selection process starts.

Once the market is primed, the detailed requirement or specification will need to be communicated in some way. For public-sector contracts, this will often be through advertising aimed at reaching either a wide range of suppliers or a more tightly defined range (for example, where a framework has already been set up – see Chapter 10). There may be governmental rules on advertising; for instance, in the European Union, all contracts over a certain value must be advertised in the *Official Journal of the European Union* (unless an existing framework established following previous advertising is being used).

If there is less interest in the assignment than expected from suppliers, it is worth finding out why this is so; for example, the requirement may be unclear or the wrong group of suppliers may have been targeted.

Stage 2: Drawing up a shortlist

If the assignment is large enough to justify a wide trawl of potential suppliers, organisations may use a pre-qualification process. Rather than issuing a formal tender document to a large number of suppliers, asking for detailed proposals, an initial sifting of suppliers is done through a less complex process – often a Pre-Qualification Questionnaire (PQQ). The primary purpose of the PQQ is to make sure that all shortlisted suppliers are capable of doing what is required. The second purpose is to help identify which of those capable of doing the job should be shortlisted.

The optimal number of suppliers to shortlist depends on the nature and complexity of the assignment, but for most single-supplier contracts 4–8 will ensure the process is sufficiently competitive while remaining manageable. Suppliers will not be keen to compete in a full tendering process if they consider the odds of winning are too long. If the aim is to appoint a framework of suppliers, the number asked to tender will depend on the size of the desired framework and whether "lots" are to be used within the framework. If a framework of five suppliers is the target, asking 8–12 firms to tender is reasonable; for a framework of ten, as many as 20 would be asked to tender.

Questions at the PQQ stage should usually focus on the following four areas:

- Do they have the capability to carry out the assignment?
- Do they have the capacity to do the work? A supplier may have the organisational capability required, but what if all the consultants with the right skills are tied up for the next six months? (Chapter 12 describes a number of ways in which capability can be assessed.)
- Are they financially robust?
- Would they be good to work with?

To arrive at a shortlist, it is often necessary to rank potential bidders for different factors to arrive at an overall ranking. Questions about capability or capacity, or approaches to areas such as sustainability, can be scored, perhaps using the marking system described in Chapter 13. The marks can be used to determine the suppliers to be asked to tender. The marking scheme must be fair and transparent; many organisations give bidders at least an outline of the evaluation process to help them understand what is required. It is always advisable (and sometimes essential) to keep a documented audit trail of selection decisions as this will help unsuccessful bidders understand why they have not been selected and help guard against allegations of unfairness, dishonesty or impropriety.

Stage 3: Inviting tenders

Once a shortlist of suppliers has been selected, the next and often final stage is commonly referred to as the invitation to tender (ITT) or quote. Shortlisted potential suppliers should be asked to explain in detail how they would carry out the assignment, and it is usual to provide them with a draft contract so they can confirm they would accept the terms and conditions.

Shortlisted firms should be asked to explain:

- their proposed methodology or approach;
- the tools and techniques they will use;
- how they will plan and manage the assignment;
- who will be working on the assignment and why they have been chosen;
- the cost and payment approaches (for example, shared risk and reward).

Stage 4: Final selection

It may be possible or desirable to decide on a single supplier with which to negotiate the contract. The alternative is to treat two or three suppliers as preferred bidders to keep some competitive tension through the final stages of negotiation and agreement of the contract (see Chapter 12). If the draft contract provided to the shortlisted firms has not raised any significant problems, gaining final agreement should not be difficult. However, if there is uncertainty concerning the contract and there are substantive points to be discussed, having more than one firm still in the frame is sensible. In the public sector, procurement regulations may preclude or restrict the ability to carry out post-tender negotiations, which might involve a favoured supplier being given a chance to undercut the lowest bidder. However, regulations usually allow discussions that are genuinely necessary for clarification.

At some stage, the purchasing organisation will ask for a "best and final offer" from the suppliers still in the frame, after which a final decision can be made on the basis of other factors that have driven the evaluation process.

Automating supplier selection

Development in the range and quality of specialist software allows elements of the supplier selection process to be automated to an increasing degree. This is often referred to as "e-sourcing", and good products are suitable for use across a wide range of spend areas, including professional services. Such software, which may also be able to record and manage contracts, orders and payment (see Chapter 8), allows purchasers and potential suppliers to share documents and communicate easily and quickly. Suppliers can submit bids, proposals or tenders electronically in a secure and controlled manner.

The tender evaluation process can also be partly automated, so that calculation of scores is carried out automatically once evaluators enter their scores for each supplier, and sensitivity analysis (for instance, looking at the effect that changing weightings or scoring has on a final evaluation result) can be carried out quickly and easily. Such systems can also provide a much stronger audit trail for evaluation decisions than a purely manual process; this is particularly important in the government sector.

However, in all but the simplest supplier selection process, human judgment is still essential in assessing what potential providers are offering and how this meets an organisation's needs. Software should help purchasers (and users) determine the best supplier, not dictate the process.

E-auctions

E-auctions or reverse auctions have been used in purchasing since the late 1990s. Buyers issue a requirement to a number of potential suppliers, who then place bids to supply the goods or services at a proposed price, usually through a real-time electronic system. The bidders are informed about the lowest bid at a point in time and have the chance to undercut it with a lower bid of their own. After a set time or when lower bids stop coming in, the lowest bidder wins the right to supply at that price. More complex auctions can include other attributes as well as price, or can seek to optimise supply across different locations or products.

Reverse auctions have proved effective in many spend areas although they are not always successful. They can, for instance, lead to poor quality if suppliers cut corners to meet prices they have bid in their enthusiasm to win the contract. They usually work better for commodities than for complex services, where reducing everything to a lowest price is therefore not simple. But although it is unlikely to be appropriate for a complex assignment, where many variables other than just price come into play, it should not be ruled out as an option where the service can be clearly defined and is of a repeatable nature, as for a standard, transactional, legal or audit process.

12 Selection criteria

George Adams is the chief executive of Spicers, Europe's leading office products company; before that he was responsible for business development at a French home improvement chain, Castorama. In both roles he has seen many consulting firms and many procurement managers at work. He divides his consulting needs into two groups:

> *If the issue is a strategic one, then we'll go to a firm we've worked with before, but if it relates to a specific functional area, we'll look for a specialist in this field so we can draw on their experience.*

The second category of consultants is easier to evaluate:

> *You want someone who can do the job. Drawing up a clear, tight specification will immediately limit the number of firms capable of doing the work. Once we've whittled potential suppliers down in this way, so that we know we have two or three which are all equally capable of doing the work, we'll then look at price and how soon they can start.*

Strategy firms pose more of a challenge:

> *It's harder to be clear about the inputs you need; what matters is the output and ensuring the business takes ownership of that output. It's about the transfer of knowledge from one side to another.*

Although price is important, value for money is more so:

> *You have a feel about how much you want to spend anyway and tend to tailor the firms you approach depending on that. Sometimes you just want the best people. If you're sensible, you tell them what price you want to pay and focus on what they can do for that budget.*

Adams believes that central purchasing teams can play a useful role when it comes to selecting a functional specialist but is sceptical of their value where more strategic work is concerned:

> *Buying this kind of consulting more cheaply isn't very helpful: you really need to know the firm you choose can do the job.*

Selecting the best professional services firm for an assignment is not always easy. Professional services assignments are often confidential; many demand a bespoke service, designed to meet a unique set of requirements, making information about past projects either hard to come by or potentially misleading. The people who deliver the services are almost always experts in a particular field, but assessing their competence is difficult unless you, too, are an expert.

The previous chapter outlined an overall selection process; this one looks in more detail at the factors to consider and the questions to ask. It focuses on three main factors – the firm, the individual advisers, and price and value for money – each of which varies in importance depending on the stage in the buying process.

The firm

The firm-related factors to consider fall into three groups: past, future and what can be described as the "halo effect". These may be taken into account at the pre-qualification stage or the invitation to tender stage in a manner that is proportionate to the size, risk and importance of the assignment.

A firm's past

Usually the first questions a professional services firm will be asked will concern its size, soundness and operations, and will be aimed at discovering facts about its staff numbers, specialisms, finances, insurance cover, and so on.

The world is full of small professional services firms and freelance advisers, and reassurance that they can do the work and will be around to complete it successfully is essential. But it is important not to raise the factual bar so high that it excludes firms which might offer excellent value for money but which, say, have not been around very long. Selection criteria should be tailored for the project in hand and not be a single, generic standard applied equally to large and small projects.

Every professional services firm possesses a range of experience and capabilities, and its track record is highly relevant: the work it has done in the field; how similar assignments have gone; the expertise and knowledge it has accumulated. Capability can be linked to experience but can also be gained through buying in staff, or via academic or other research.

The three most important tools for assessing a firm's experience or capability are as follows:

- Case studies that can indicate whether the firm has completed similar engagements in the past.
- Evidence of its technical knowledge and ability to think around a given subject.
- References from clients – even though firms will put forward clients who are likely to provide a favourable reference. To get round this it may be possible to tap into contacts who can give an objective view, or firms can be asked to outline similar assignments over recent years and give permission for clients to be contacted, subject to guarantees about confidentiality.

All three tools can be useful at this stage, but it is important to understand that they help establish a firm's credentials and not those of the individuals who will work on the project.

A project's future

The criteria above are backward-looking; they focus on what the supplier has built (financial stability), done (experience) and learnt (capability). Equally important is to look forwards and to explore how a firm proposes to carry out the assignment.

Experience and capability count for nothing if they are not relevant to the work in hand. Indeed, one of the complaints clients make about the proposals produced by professional services firms is that they can appear generic, as if they have been wheeled out for earlier sales pitches. Professional services firms should demonstrate that they have listened to and understood the requirements, and have adapted their approach to satisfy them. In making their pitch they should run through what they understand the scope and focus of the work to be. Their proposal should include:

- details of their approach and what they will be doing;
- the kind of people they are proposing for the work;

- evidence of the necessary qualifications and/or experience;
- evidence that the approach as outlined will deliver the outcome.

In the private sector, a firm's proposed solution is often given less weight than its prior experience. In the public sector, regulations can push buyers towards reliance on the former. Every project should involve an assessment of the relative importance of experience, capability and the proposed solution. The more standard an assignment, the more experience can be relied upon; the more novel and non-standard a piece of work is, the more important the underlying capability and the proposed solution are.

The halo effect

Brands are as important in professional services as they are in other sectors. As with so many consumer products, familiar names are comforting. They also, as that old adage "no one gets sacked for choosing IBM" so neatly illustrates, provide a means to justify a selection to colleagues. Because brand visibility (or lack of it) cannot be ignored, it makes sense to make it explicit in the decision-making process. How important is it to the project? Is the work so politically sensitive, so high-profile internally or externally, that stakeholders will take comfort in the fact that a well-known firm has been brought in? If that is not the case, looking for an "unbranded" firm may save a great deal of money.

Reputation is slightly different. A firm that does not have a well-known brand name may still have an excellent reputation among its clients because they sing its praises without being prompted. In a transparent market, such information would be easy to come by – through a professional services equivalent of eBay or Trip Advisor ratings – but in the absence of that an organisation may have to rely on:

- canvassing the opinion of colleagues;
- exploiting contacts;
- asking the professional services firm to provide a list of five past clients to speak to – the speed with which a firm responds to such a request says a lot about it;
- contacting someone who used to work for the firm. This can give a good insight into its culture because employee relationships are often the mirror images of client relationships – if a firm is bad at communicating with its employees, it is probably bad at communicating with its clients.

All of the above can be incorporated into formal evaluation processes, as can a firm's corporate social responsibility programme or quality processes, client surveys, staff remuneration and how much it is dependent on satisfying clients or selling. A firm's actions count for more than its words.

Individual advisers

Many of the factors referred to above relate to the individuals who work for a firm. The financial and operational make-up of the firm, its brand and the extent to which its reputation is built on company policies are, indeed, revealing. But experience, capability and to a large extent reputation rest on the individual advisers the firm employs, and it is the individuals who will be working on a project that matter when it comes to pruning a shortlist to one or two firms. The selection process must include a chance to assess the individuals who will be assigned to the project.

Getting access to those people should not be a problem, yet a common complaint of clients of professional services firms is that the people they met to discuss the project were not the people who worked on it. This is usually the result of habit and logistics rather than conspiracy. The way a professional services firm is structured gives it an economic incentive to focus senior people on sales rather than delivery and to keep people busy, so any delays in getting an assignment off the ground can mean that people who would or might have been involved are assigned to other projects. Because this is common, there needs to be absolute clarity about who will work on the project and how much time they will put into it.

Once it has been established who will be on the team they need to be met, ideally in circumstances as close to real work as possible. Presentations by shortlisted firms or "beauty parades" are a fast and efficient way to get an overview of each firm's approach and to judge the overall quality of the individuals being put forward. But the somewhat artificial environment in which the formal presentations take place means they should be supplemented by:

- interviewing the advisers as though vetting them for a job;
- arranging sessions involving the advisers and the internal team they will be working with to gauge the overall chemistry;
- asking them to do a pilot piece of work – most firms, especially for larger projects, will be willing to do some unpaid work and this will help evaluate the way they work and their output;

- giving them a tight deadline to complete something so you can also see how they operate under pressure;
- bringing the shortlisted firms (or a subset of them) together for a workshop. Some may complain that they do not want to give away proprietary information to their competitors, but the best firms know that methodologies are things to be built on, not crutches to rely on.

What makes a good adviser?

This is one of those "how long is a piece of string" questions, as the answer depends on the project and personal preferences. An adviser who gets on well with one client may not hit it off with another.

There are, however, generic qualities to look for:

- **Technical knowledge.** Whatever is required the advisers must have.
- **Logical thinking.** Being able to analyse data and the facts and make decisions based on them.
- **Listening skills.** A common complaint about professional advisers is that they think they know better than their clients. The best advisers, who may indeed be leading ones, will always listen carefully to a client rather than leap to a conclusion.
- **Discipline and organisational skills.** The ability to organise work efficiently, to follow up on actions promptly and assiduously, and to keep track of decisions and actions is essential. There is little point working with advisers who are only good at throwing in new ideas or challenging existing assumptions: things need to be done.

Well-known techniques such as Myers-Briggs (which analyses individuals' preferred ways of working) and Belbin (which identifies the roles people are likely to play when they work in a team) can provide invaluable feedback on how well a team will get on. There are three attitudes to investigate when assessing the personal chemistry of the client-adviser relationship:

- **Past/present versus future.** Whether the client or the potential advisers focus on what has happened, what is happening at the moment, or the future.
- **Problems versus opportunities.** How the client or the potential advisers think about things – glass half full or half empty.

◼ **"Big picture" versus detail.** Whether the client or the potential advisers need all the facts before making a decision or prefer to take a "helicopter view".

None of the above is right or wrong, but if attitudes do not align or complement they may cause the relationships to crack. The chemistry must be right if the client-adviser relationship is to be successful, which is why it is common for people to take their advisers with them when they change jobs. A purchasing manager may worry that an overly close personal relationship is coming into play, but if the client knows that this adviser is competent, and that they can work together well and happily, the client's desire to retain that adviser is perfectly understandable; purchasing staff need to be sensitive to that.

Price and value for money

Price plays an important part in the purchasing of professional services, but not necessarily in the way that might be expected. It helps to:

◼ identify a market rate and exclude "outlying" suppliers;
◼ put a value on what a firm provides above and beyond that provided by the individual advisers;
◼ provide a basis on which discounts can be negotiated in the final stages of negotiation.

Usually in professional services, the amount paid has a direct impact on the quality of what is provided. If a firm is asked to cut its rates by half, that may mean it will use less experienced, cheaper staff to do the work. But price should not be automatically equated with quality – firm A (a big firm) may charge more for its staff because it has high overheads and because its brand may provide some degree of quality assurance. Firm B is much smaller but it recruits people who have left firm A so the calibre of its staff is not dissimilar. Firm B, however, has lower overheads and its brand cannot support premium prices. The quality it provides is comparable to that provided by firm A, but its prices will be lower. In general, lower prices have an impact on quality only when a purchaser seeks to extract a higher than expected discount.

Two points should be weighed up when considering price:

◼ To what extent is the service required highly customised and heavily dependent on the calibre of the people who deliver it?

◪ At what point does the negotiable discount tip over into something that will erode the quality of the service delivered?

The market rate

One of the ramifications of a lack of transparency in professional services is that is difficult to judge market rates. For standardised services, it is possible to find out what other organisations pay, but for non-standard assignments making price comparisons is difficult. In the absence of objective measures, prices can be compared using two criteria:

◪ **Expectations.** Everyone has an amount of money in mind that they are prepared to pay, whether that is a budget set in advance, a sense of how much a project costs and/or an estimate of what it is worth. A purchaser looks for firms that match that expectation because it suggests that they are thinking on the same lines. It follows that the purchaser will exclude firms that are much more expensive or extremely cheap on the grounds that they cannot have understood the brief.

◪ **Other firms.** Potential suppliers can be asked to estimate what a project will cost and these estimates can be compared. Although much maligned by professional services firms, asking firms to enter online bids in an e-auction can be an effective way to do this. From the information provided it is possible to see the range of prices and, because the bidders usually have a chance to adjust their prices based on comparisons with other bidders, the point at which they start to converge becomes apparent.

The market rate is therefore something that should be considered at an early stage, if only to be able to move on to other factors. Having excluded the firms that do not meet expectations or are way above or below the average fees, the different services on offer can be compared.

Valuing a firm versus an individual

Price helps assess how much the firm-related factors cost on top of what the individual advisers would cost. The larger the professional services firm, the higher its fees are likely to be. This is partly to recoup its higher expenses, but it is also a reflection of the brand: it is the premium paid for working with the firm. Price highlights this differential, making it easier to decide whether a firm is worth it.

A good deal

Many buyers adopt a negotiating strategy that keeps a couple of suppliers in the frame before the final decision is made. Knowing they are in competition sharpens suppliers' commercial sensibilities and makes them more likely to be flexible in the final stages of closing the deal than they would be if they were the only firm in the running. However, the most important aspect of a good deal is value, not price. Assuming that the remaining firms are offering similar prices and a comparable standard of service, the final stages of the buying cycle may be better used to extract more from them than to beat them down in price.

The inevitable compromise

No supplier scores highest across all the evaluation criteria. The only way to resolve the inevitable trade-offs is to be clear about the reasons for hiring a professional services firm. For specialist skills, a suitably qualified small firm or independent adviser may make sense. Similarly, for a short project, worrying about the long-term financial sustainability of a small firm does not make sense. But if the project is sufficiently large or high-profile to warrant the involvement of a big, branded firm, the "price" of that may depend on the depth of specialist skills available. What is wanted? Which firms and/or individual advisers can provide it? How much are you willing to pay?

Getting the balance right

Telecommunications firm BT recently went through a radical revamp of its supplier selection process and selection criteria with the aim of reducing the number of suppliers it uses and cutting costs, without cutting itself off from the specialist skills it needs access to. The following section outlines how the firm went about achieving the balance it sought.

BT Group

In 2008 BT, one of the world's leading providers of communications solutions and services, reviewed its procurement arrangements under which its supply base had proliferated. In consulting alone, during the 2007/08 financial year BT's operational stakeholders had initiated contractual relationships with over 200 companies, the majority of which worked on single projects, generating a long "tail". With recession starting to bite, BT's procurement team were asked to reduce the number of suppliers and cut expenditure on consultants, while ensuring that the company still had access to the specialist skills it needed.

The introduction a year or so earlier of a new authorisation system, Camera Consulting, helped, as this allowed expenditure on all professional services to be tracked and managed more effectively. However, project owners still tended to input their requirements on the system only after they had selected a supplier and agreed the commercial arrangements.

When Paul Vincent took over as procurement director for consultancy and professional services in July 2007, the focus of the team he inherited had become largely reactive. They were knee-deep in 11th hour/retrospective contractual negotiations and no priority was given to mining the management information that would shine a light on where they could add value to the overall procurement process. Vincent says:

Every month, my team extracted a report of those projects that had started before the purchase order had been issued to the supplier. This report went to a finance co-ordinating point but we had no involvement in its distribution or in any discussions that subsequently ensued.

Vincent initiated a review of the entire process for buying consulting services, starting with analysis of the data in Camera:

For the next three months, I primarily focused on improving the effectiveness with which my team worked with the rest of BT's business and took a number of steps to improve their visibility and general proactivity. I also instigated a review of how consultancy was defined and what the quantifiable project benefits were.

In September 2007, Vincent was joined by Stephen Hayers, who took over as vice-president for services procurement. Hayers immediately initiated his own review across all the areas for which he was responsible to identify where a strategic sourcing initiative – one that aggregated expenditure and maximised commercial leverage – would yield the greatest dividends. From the work that Vincent and his team had already started, it was clear that there was considerable scope for changing the way BT bought consulting services. Hayers recalls:

There was an opportunity here to make significant savings. Our aim was to create and implement a world-class sourcing strategy for this category.

Their efforts received further support from a BT-wide procurement transformation programme that was launched the following November by Neil

Rogers, the chief procurement officer. Internally branded as "trACTION", the aim of this initiative was to make sure BT's procurement function was fully aligned within the company as a whole and focused on supporting the strategic business priorities. The trACTION programme contained a number of work streams, ranging from an overhaul of category strategies to the management of spend information to supplier relationship management.

By December, Hayers and Vincent were in a position to pass on the results of the analysis of consulting expenditure to chief financial officers across BT's business and by February 2008 had gained their commitment to a different approach:

☑ reducing expenditure, largely through better demand management;
☑ establishing an approved supplier list (ASL) that would provide BT with the expertise it needed on market-leading commercial terms.

Table 12.1 **BT's decision-making framework for consultancy and professional services expenditure**

	Objective	Role of the line of business	Role of the procurement
1	Obtain a clear view of upcoming requirements	Provide information on likely needs	Provide monthly management information on spend, current supplier performance and compliance
2	Qualify projects and obtain CFO authorisation	Specify why external support is needed and what the measurable outcomes will be	Redesign the Camera system to provide an automated mechanism for managing demand
3	Ensure the appropriate expertise is bought at the best commercial rates	Use the ASL for around 95% of requirements, except where specialist subcontractors are required by BT's external customers	Create and manage a ASL for consultancy and professional services in which commercial arrangement focuses on outcomes, not inputs
4	Manage projects and supplier relationships	Manage the consultancy relationship on an individual basis	Maintain a consolidated view of the work being carried out by BT's ASL suppliers
5	Ensure projects are effectively concluded	Confirm that the outcomes sought have been delivered	Manage the post-project review process

The new framework comprised five main stages, each of which required the procurement team and their internal customers (the "lines of business") to work together (Table 12.1).

Vincent says:

The key was to create a decision-making framework, not a procurement process. What we wanted was a road map for managing expenditure on consulting from the point at which the need for consultants was identified to the conclusion of the project.

Table 12.2 **BT's selection criteria**

Stage	Criteria applied
Pre-qualification	Be interested in working as a supplier for BT.
	Agree to BT's payment, intellectual property rights and insurance terms.
Request for information	Stakeholder feedback: including service, quality, innovation, and the overall relationship.
	Pricing: suppliers complete a questionnaire that forms the baseline from which cost savings are measured.
	Terms: an assessment of the extent to which firms complied with BT's operational controls.
	Technical capability: how firms differentiate themselves from their competitors, delivery of successful projects supported by references and case studies.
Request for proposal	Stakeholder feedback: principal users were involved in the evaluation and decision-making process.
	Commercial: based on rate cards, discounts and rebates offered.
	Contractual: agreement to BT's standard terms and conditions and supporting schedules.
	Technical capability: how consultancy firms differentiate themselves from their competitors and demonstrate what they are bidding for, evidenced by case studies and references.
	Track record in the telecoms industry: demonstrated through case studies.
	Quality and service: consultants' service must be of consistently high quality. Service appropriateness and responsiveness are measured through periodic supplier performance reviews. Preference is given to firms with a history of providing outstanding service and quality based on their customer references and case studies.
	Value added services: consultants are encouraged to be creative and develop suggestions on enhancing the BT relationship, quality, service levels and cost efficiencies.

The new decision-making framework was implemented over the course of the next eight months. Vincent says:

We then got on with rebuilding the preferred supplier list. That meant filtering out those suppliers who didn't meet BT's basic terms, detailed in our pre-qualification questionnaire, and, even more generally, those who weren't actually consultants at all.

This stage of the sourcing exercise, combined with a tighter definition of what was meant by consulting, reduced the list of suppliers from 566 to about 270.

Next, Vincent and his colleagues sent out a request for information (RFI), asking firms to agree to expanded terms and to provide evidence of their capability. Responses to this were filtered according to an evaluation of supplier performance, feedback from stakeholders, compliance criteria (see Table 12.2) and an evaluation of supplier capabilities using a customised/tailor-made methodology. The result was a list reduced to 106 (from 270) suppliers, who then received a request for proposal (RFP). The final stage in the process was an e-auction.

BT is keen to maintain an intelligent relationship with its ASL, recognising that, as business conditions change, the list needs to be reviewed to take account of new suppliers with whom agreements are desirable and existing suppliers with whom a formalised relationship is no longer appropriate.

Hayers summarises the initiative:

There are few procurement category initiatives that can claim to have had the same level of business impact that this one did. Not only did the team overhaul the complete approach to sourcing consultancy within BT, but they did it by transforming the perceived level of value added offered by the procurement function. All through the programme we ensured that the business did not feel "done to" and we arrived at an approved list of suppliers that the business wanted to work with. We have seen compliance with our ASL grow from 30% to 94% with the associated benefits to our business and the suppliers on our ASL.

13 Scoring bids and tenders

When considering different methods for scoring bids and tenders, there are two important points to bear in mind:

- Ask questions and evaluate responses only in areas that are important to the assignment. If a consultant is to write a report on potential acquisitions in Armenia, skills transfer may not be of the slightest interest, so do not ask about it or evaluate it. Innovation may not be important when buying a standard service and should not be an evaluation criterion in that case.
- Small changes in the evaluation method can inadvertently sway the balance from one supplier to another.

Some organisations take a scientific and systematic approach to scoring bids, which makes it easier to scrutinise their decision-making process. Others, essentially in the private sector, prefer to rely on judgment.

Non-price evaluation criteria

The questions asked in a tender document will relate to either non-price factors (such as quality or service levels) or price/cost factors. The purchasing organisation should decide which non-price factors or criteria are important for the assignment. What are the most important attributes that a supplier must have? Is it specialist knowledge, a high level of responsiveness, or just a basic quality level and low prices? Examples of such criteria are outlined in Chapter 12. The selected criteria then form the basis for the evaluation and for the selection of the best supplier for that work.

Each question in a tender document should relate to one, and only one, evaluation criterion. This makes scoring simpler, more direct, and avoids having to read an entire response document to dig out references for each criterion.

A simple and direct question might be: "Explain the quality processes to be used during this assignment and how they will add value to the outputs supplied." This can be marked directly against the "quality" evaluation criterion, assuming there is one.

However, the request might be: "Describe the methodology, tools and techniques to be used for the assignment, including project and quality plans." This may sound good, but if "methodology", "quality processes" and "project management" are three separate evaluation criteria (which is quite possible), it will probably be difficult to score each of them from this single request.

The evaluation system should be as simple as possible. There are many scoring systems for marking responses; the one shown in Table 13.1 (or something similar) is manageable and results in clear differentiation between bidders.

Table 13.1 **Scoring system for assessing invitation to tender responses**

Score	Criteria
5	Meets all requirements and offers some added value
4	Meets all the main requirements
3	Generally meets all the main requirements with some minor exceptions
2	Meets some requirements with a few large gaps or exceptions
1	Meets few requirements; serious concerns
0	Does not meet any requirements; fails to answer the question

For substantial assignments, some organisations construct a "model" response: the answer for each question that would score five out of five. This can help identify a benchmark. Ideally, more than one evaluator should mark each proposal. A moderator or evaluation board can then make sure that there are no discrepancies in the marking across bids and evaluators. Records should be kept of the process and there should be a clear audit trail.

The price question

Scoring non-price factors is more straightforward than scoring price. Following a non-price evaluation process like that described above, a buyer might start with a table similar to Table 13.2.

The data could be used to produce a chart (see Figure 13.1 on page 138). Any scores below a predetermined minimum might be excluded, on the grounds that an overall score of, say, less than 50% on non-price factors meant the supplier was simply not up to the task, whatever the cost (the dotted line on the chart represents this cut-off). A more sophisticated approach could have a cut-off based on a single criterion. It is good practice to inform suppliers of critical questions or criteria.

Table 13.2 **An evaluation process: the starting point**

Supplier	Total non-price score (%)	Cost ($m)
A	54	10
B	84	12
C	96	13
D	66	13

The chart could be used as the basis for discussion by the tender board, evaluation panel or steering group. The starting point would be that the lowest cost bid above the minimum standard would be the winner, and the discussion would focus on whether the additional cost of other bids could be justified by the additional non-price "score". In other words, is it worth paying another million pounds to get better quality service, a more flexible approach or whatever factors have affected the higher score?

In Table 13.2, supplier A offers the lowest price and has passed the overall quality threshold (predefined as a 50% score); if below that level, it would have been automatically eliminated, however low its price was. Supplier D cannot win, both because its bid is more expensive than Supplier B's and because it scores less on non-price factors than any of the other suppliers. But should B or even C be chosen over A: is it worth paying another $2m for the extra 30 "points" of non-price? Similarly, is it then worth paying a further $1m to move from B to C to gain the extra 12 points?

Good decisions can be made through this process, but it still contains an element of subjectivity, and the price/non-price trade-offs are not based on specific weighting or marking systems. Purchasing staff, particularly in the public sector, have come under more pressure to develop clearer evaluation mechanisms to legitimise and formalise the judgmental process described above. Recent challenges to supplier selection decisions in the public sector, some successful, are increasingly focusing on the detail of the evaluation process. For example, in 2008 *Supply Management Magazine* reported that a High Court judge in Northern Ireland had ordered the cancellation of an £800m ($1,250m) construction framework agreement after procurement rules were broken. The decision followed a legal challenge by a building company that came sixth in a tender to find five suppliers for a four-year framework to provide construction services for urban regeneration, further education, arts and sports developments. The Central Procurement Directorate, which ran the tender process, broke the rules by not disclosing to suppliers the subcriteria and weightings it used to evaluate the bids.

Some technique needs to be used to score price and then combine price and non-price scores together in a consistent, reasonable and robust manner. One approach would be to use the concept of utility, converting price and all other factors into a "utility" score, which is potentially different for every company, and even every contract. In practice, except perhaps for big procurement exercises, this is probably too complex.

In the three simpler methods of scoring price described below, price is marked on a scale of 0–100, and then half that score (a 50% weighting) is added to half the non-price score to reach an overall score.

Percentage scoring

This method usually involves scoring the lowest cost bid as 100. So in the example above, A scores 100. B is 20% more expensive so it scores 80, 20% less than A (Table 13.3). C is 30% more expensive so it scores 70, 30% less than A. (Supplier D has been disregarded for the reasons explained above.)

Table 13.3 **Percentage-based scoring**

Supplier	Quality	Weighted (50%)	Cost ($m)	Price score (see scales in text)	Weighted (50%)	Total
A	54	27	10	100	50	77
B	84	42	12	80	40	82
C	96	48	13	70	35	83

The method is simple and apparently fair, but it has disadvantages. A 10% cost difference may not sound much but may represent a huge amount of money and a score only 10% lower than the cheaper bid may not reflect that adequately. Moreover, even an extremely high bid may score quite well. A variant of this method is to apply a price curve or a multiplying factor to the score, so that every percentage point of additional price loses the bidder more than one percentage point of score. So a price 20% above the cheapest could be scored at 20 × 2 or 40% lower than the cheapest bid (so it scores 60 out of 100 rather than the original

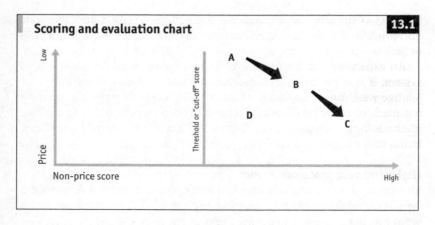

Scoring and evaluation chart | 13.1

80). This places more emphasis on price and means that higher prices are "punished" more dramatically.

Scoring by rank

Using this method, the highest-priced supplier scores 0 and the lowest-priced scores 100. The others are placed at equal increments between. So if there were six suppliers, they would score respectively 0, 20, 40, 60, 80 and 100 points. This uses the full range of scores available and distinguishes between different costs. But it is fundamentally unfair because the scores could exaggerate the difference between two suppliers whose bids are only a few dollars apart. It also distorts the weighting. Non-price scoring based on the sort of marking scheme outlined above results in most suppliers scoring somewhere between, say, 50% and 80%. Thus only a fraction, perhaps one-third of the possible scale, is used, so when combined with a price scoring system that uses the whole 0–100 scale

Table 13.4 **Scoring by rank**

Supplier	Quality	Weighted (50%)	Cost ($m)	Price score (see scales in text)	Weighted (50%)	Total
A	54	27	10	100	50	77
B	84	42	12	50	25	67
C	96	48	13	0	0	48

(Table 13.4), the effect is to amplify the weighting of cost compared with non-price. A 50% weighting for cost becomes, in effect, more like a 70% or 80% weighting.

An expensive bid, however strong the quality, cannot win under this system. If non-price is also scored on a ranking system, the problem of relative weighting is avoided; however, the problem of unfairness is then repeated for non-price factors. These disadvantages should rule out this methodology, although it has been used for some important tenders. Using this method, A comes out a clear winner.

Highest/lowest conceivable price

This method introduces a somewhat artificial construct, but it has some significant advantages. It relies on specifying a marking scale based on what has been decided to be the highest and lowest conceivable prices. The highest conceivable price can usually be defined in terms of the budget available for the procurement. What is the most that could be paid? If the answer is $15m, any higher bid should score 0 for cost, or be eliminated. (As budgets are rarely set in stone, the 0 score could be set at 10% above the budget.) At the other extreme, what is the lowest possible price that might be achieved? If it is $7.5 million, this would score 100. This is then designated as the "100" score. Table 13.5 shows how the bids score on that linear $7.5m–15m scale, with B emerging as the winner.

Table 13.5 **Scoring price against a predetermined scale**

Supplier	Quality	Weighted (50%)	Cost ($m)	Price score (see scales in text)	Weighted (50%)	Total
A	54	27	10	66	33	60
B	84	42	12	40	20	62
C	96	48	13	26	13	61

This method reflects "utility" quite well, in that high bids can be "punished", but the scoring is less extreme than in the scoring by rank method. It will often lead to scores around the 50–75% mark, which matches well with the normal non-price range, although in the example here a wider range of non-price scores has been used to demonstrate the different methodologies more clearly. But bids that are close score similarly, which would seem to be a prerequisite of a fair system.

A big "but"

Using the three different scoring methods described, suppliers A, B and C can all win the contract. This demonstrates the importance of taking a view about the importance of price and price differentials and deciding which method is most appropriate in the circumstances.

As Victor Gaybadullin's comments illustrate (see below), organisations vary in the importance they attach to price in evaluating bids from professional services firms. On some occasions it will be a major factor in the decision; on others, particularly where scarce expertise is sought or a relationship with a particular supplier is already in place, it will have little bearing.

Buying human resources consulting

Based in Moscow, Victor Gaybadullin has worked in senior HR roles at Zurich Financial Services and Perekriostok. In his experience, the decision to hire consultants is based on whether or not the skills required are available in-house:

> In the large organisations I've worked in, we would use consultants for work we didn't have the capacity to do ourselves, such as long-range planning after a merger or acquisition, or assessing our top managers. In such cases, we'd simply invite some of the big, well-known firms to submit proposals, and make a decision based not so much on price, but on our long-term relationship with the firm, the quality of work they'd done in the past, their presence in the local market, and sometimes political reasons. For example, when it came to assessing our top managers on one occasion, I had to use a particular firm because the business had already bought an assessment tool from them, even though they were twice as expensive as the firm I wanted to use. For smaller organisations, price is more important: they can't afford the services of brand name consulting companies and have to work with less famous, or even no-name, firms.

In selecting a firm, Gaybadullin and his colleagues would consider the firm's reputation, its range of services, its experience in the area where the services were needed, its industry knowledge, evidence of successful projects elsewhere and whether the firm had the capacity to resource what in some cases were large projects adequately:

But we would always look at both the firm and the individual. Sometimes even a no-name consulting company can provide high-quality services if they specialise in a particular area or industry.

If the project was large, it made sense to build up internal capacity, rather than relying on consultants:

When we needed to carry out a massive assessment of line managers in Perekriostok, we calculated the costs involved and decided to create our own, internal assessment centre. In such cases, price is critical and any other competencies of a consulting firm are not taken into account. It's just too expensive – let's do it ourselves.

Although much of his experience has been with international companies, Gaybadullin has also seen how Russian organisations buy professional services, and how that has changed over time:

A big company with an existing international presence or with plans to expand abroad will generally behave like any other international company, using the standard procedure of central procurement with a tender process, several applicants, terms of references, standard proposals, presentations, negotiations, and so on. A local Russian firm will tend to use a simple process, especially if it's based outside Moscow. For example, in Ufa (a city of 1m inhabitants) there are only two local consulting companies, so the choice is simple: make a decision to buy or not to buy external consulting and then, at the most, invite these two companies for their presentation. Nowadays in Russia the process of buying consulting services is becoming a part of the business planning process, when we're planning our resources for any day-to-day or development activities. Thus, it's hard to spend any money that is not in the plan even if it's obvious that it will lead to positive results. Due to the crisis, the price is becoming more important in negotiations and decision-making while choosing the consulting firm and central procurement people are more involved in the process of buying – that's one of the overall tendencies in the Russian market.

PART 5
NEGOTIATION AND CONTRACTING

Once a shortlist of potential professional services firms has been narrowed down to one or possibly two contenders, it is time to focus on negotiating the final terms. This can be trickier than with other types of services for a number of reasons. The organisational structure of most professional services firms can make it hard to determine who has the authority to negotiate, and a purchasing team may find its negotiating hand weakened because the decision to use a particular firm has already been made by senior management. Furthermore, concrete data and standard definitions can be hard to come by; even if a firm divulges its standard rates, reliable sources of comparative information may be scarce. Negotiating positions can, however, be strengthened by a good understanding of how the pyramid structure, which underpins almost all professional firms, drives costs, and different approaches to pricing.

14 Negotiation

Negotiation is sometimes seen as a battle of wills or intellects. However, at the core of *Getting to Yes*, by Roger Fisher, William Ury and Bruce Patton, is the belief in the power of "principled negotiation" or "negotiation on the merits". This attempts to defuse the personal and sometimes confrontational nature of negotiation with the aim of achieving, so far as possible, a win-win situation for both parties. Their approach highlights four elements:

- **People.** People should be separated from the problem to avoid confusing the aims of the negotiation with personal position and feelings of the negotiating "opponents". Negotiation should be seen as a joint problem-solving activity rather than a contest of wills or intelligence.
- **Interests.** Successful negotiation comes from focusing on interests not positions. Positions are where the negotiators stand on an argument; interests are what they are seeking to get out of the negotiation.
- **Options.** Good negotiators will consider a variety of possibilities before deciding what to do. They look for options which are attractive in different ways to each party – for instance, suggesting that an assignment could provide a useful case study for a consulting firm may encourage the firm to take on work at a lower than usual price.
- **Criteria.** It must be possible to assess the negotiating outcome. As far as possible, negotiation should be founded on facts rather than opinions or prejudice. For example, simply telling a firm its day rates are too expensive is likely to be less successful than comparing them with benchmark rates of other comparable firms.

The BATNA concept

An important concept in *Getting to Yes* is the "BATNA": the Best Alternative To a Negotiated Agreement. This is what might be termed the fallback position should negotiations with a desired supplier fail. If several lawyers are lined up, all of whom are available and capable of doing the required work, the BATNA is strong and a firm line can be taken in the negotiation safe in the knowledge that a good alternative is available should negotiations with one of the possible lawyers not work out. If a lawyer is the only one in the world who can do the work and is much in demand, the BATNA and the negotiating hand are weak.

The perception of the BATNA is as important as the actual BATNA. If a supplier believes a buyer's BATNA is strong (even if it is not), it will behave in a certain manner.

Distributive and collaborative negotiation

Another book, *Essentials of Negotiation*, by three North American-based academics, Roy Lewicki, David Saunders and John Barry, makes a clear distinction between distributive and collaborative negotiation. At times, a negotiation may not have the scope for a comfortable win-win situation, which is the aim in collaborative negotiation. Or there may be little benefit in giving away some value to the other party. If a buyer is purchasing a used vehicle from someone they will never see again, why shouldn't they push for a price that is unfair for the seller? If an organisation is never going to use a consultant again, why not push for the best possible deal? There is a single cake of fixed size, and the parties negotiate to see how large a slice each will get. If one party gets more, the other gets less. This style of negotiation is generally termed "distributive bargaining" as it relates to how in effect a fixed "prize" is distributed between the negotiating parties. If you get a better deal, your opponent loses out.

Professional services negotiations should generally be collaborative in style. A distributive, "winner takes all" negotiating approach is rarely appropriate. This is because:

- The potential outcome of most professional services assignments can be positive or negative. So negotiations should seek to improve the likelihood of a positive outcome, which often means what might be termed "concessions" in the interests of securing a long-term benefit. For example, a bonus scheme may be negotiated that links the amount of bonus paid to elements of the desired outcome, such as quality, delivery dates, and so on.
- Most professional services assignments involve the two parties working closely with each other (Part 6 discusses contract and supplier management in more detail) and a distributive negotiating style risks undermining the all-important working relationship before the assignment has even started.

- It is relatively easy for professional services firms to recover the ground they have lost in negotiations. They may do this by adjusting the level of resources they put into the project, and by taking a more rigorous line than they might otherwise have on time recording and billing, and on charging expenses. This can all be done without crossing the line that defines "unprofessional behaviour" and illustrates the downside of negotiating away the goodwill of a professional services provider.

- It is often difficult to know how good the final "product" of a professional services assignment is or how much effort and commitment has been applied. Again, a high level of goodwill and motivation on the part of the provider makes all the difference – and is something to be kept firmly in mind during negotiations.

Although a collaborative approach is likely to bring better results, negotiations should be robust. That earnings for partners in top law and consulting firms have reached such high levels is no doubt attributable in part to poor negotiating by purchasers of professional services.

Ten rules for negotiating

1 Plan – planning should account for 80% of the negotiation process.
2 Have a clear idea of what is wanted from the negotiations from the start: price, other contractual points, additional benefits.
3 Develop the negotiating strategy in advance. What is the BATNA? Can it be strengthened? What degree of flexibility in the strategy is acceptable?
4 Remember that a win-win collaborative negotiating approach is usually more fruitful.
5 Develop a good understanding of the other party's position and BATNA.
6 Negotiate with someone who has the necessary level of decision-making authority.
7 Develop alternatives and options that will appeal, for different reasons, to both parties.
8 Do not give away too much too quickly. Seek to achieve the best possible outcome, rather than one that would be reasonable.
9 Keep the "personal" out of the negotiations. If things are not going well, make the "offer" the problem, not the person making the offer.
10 Do not stop negotiating once you have achieved your main aim – for example, on day rates. What else might be available?

Important aspects

Identifying the decision-maker

Only someone with decision-making authority can make concessions or respond to new options. With professional services, it can be difficult to identify the real decision-maker; a purchaser may be talking to someone who appears to be (or is) senior and may assume that this individual has the authority to negotiate. This may not be the case, so it is crucial early in the negotiating process to establish the status of the "opposing" negotiators and to make sure that those who take part in the negotiations have genuine decision-making authority.

Getting the right information

Asymmetrical information – the situation where one party to the negotiation has greater useful knowledge about the true facts under negotiation than the other – often makes it impossible for there to be genuine collaborative negotiation. If a potential services provider says that an admired consultant is not available, but another one is more competent in that area anyway, is this true? And if the provider adds that the buyer must move quickly because demand for experts in renewable energy generation is taking off in East Asia, is this a helpful insight or a tactic to get the contract signed quickly, without proper due diligence? These examples highlight the importance of market and supplier research, and having a good understanding of how the professional services industry works.

This need for understanding applies equally to those selling professional services. Alan Thomson, who was a general manager at Reebok around the world, has sat both sides of the negotiating table on many occasions. He says:

> When I'm buying professional services, I try and make sure
> I understand the businesses I'm dealing with. But I am often
> amazed how little their people understand my business – or even
> their own sometimes. When this is the case, there is every chance
> I will just reject that firm; but if I am still interested, their lack of
> knowledge gives me a huge negotiating advantage.

Strengthening your position

In professional services purchasers often end up in a weak position because:

- The purchaser does not have time to work on a BATNA or is

presented with a *fait accompli* by the supplier and/or the user, often because one or both of them wish to avoid real competition for the work in question.

- There may be genuinely limited competition. This firm may be the world's leading expert on some arcane branch of maritime insurance law. This consultant may be the only one in Latin America who can get this software working well in the next two weeks. If the need is great enough, the feeling may be that this supplier is needed "at any cost". Again there is no credible alternative.

To ensure that a strong BATNA can be developed, there must be time to develop feasible alternatives. There must therefore be early purchaser involvement in the process; being brought into the picture the day before a multimillion-dollar negotiation is not helpful.

Learning how to handle experts

Experts usually have a good idea of their own worth, and they understand their market and their position within it. If the purchaser comes on too strong, they may decide they do not want to work with that client and will be confident that another client will be happy to pay their "usual fee". It is therefore sensible to consider what will appeal and attract the expert to taking on the assignment: perhaps that the work is interesting, a willingness to be a reference site, or the option to spread the work over a longer period of time.

Negotiating from weakness

Purchasing staff are often involved in negotiations with professional services firms only after a supplier has been chosen by the budget holder, giving the purchasing team little chance to plan and prepare or investigate alternative suppliers.

One senior purchasing manager at an international construction company gave an account of such a situation:

> I called my account manager from the consulting firm. I told him that I couldn't approve the contract. There were no clear deliverables in the proposal and the firm was not taking any real risk. The rates were high for the market and the type of work, and it wasn't clear we would get the intellectual property we needed. He initially refused to negotiate – it was a done deal with our managing director as far as he was concerned.

The purchasing manager was in some difficulty. She probably did not understand the firm's capability in the consulting area as she had not been involved. Her BATNA was poor, and she appeared to have little to offer the provider in terms of options that might get concessions in a negotiation:

> I decided I had to persuade the firm I did have something to offer. I worked to create at least the impression of a BATNA that was better than it really was. I suggested I had the power to stop the contract going though, or at least delay it, which was debatable but got the provider's attention. Then we looked at what we could offer that might get concessions in return. For instance, offering them a place on our approved supplier list; the chance to make this project into a case study or reference site that might lead to other business; and introductions to other parts of the firm. I also made it clear that if they wouldn't play ball, I would make it my life's work to ensure they never worked with our organisation again.

These tactics led to significant movement from the provider, some genuine negotiation and a much more balanced deal. Day rates proved immovable, but there was a much clearer statement of what would be delivered and by when, the firm took on part of the risk and the intellectual property issue was resolved. Clearly, a better overall purchasing process would have been preferable; but effective negotiation can improve a difficult position.

Other tactics in weak positions are to use emotions or emotion-based techniques (such as neuro-linguistic programming, see page 80) to persuade the other party to give concessions. These softer negotiation skills can be effective, although in general business negotiations are more structured and fact based than personal negotiations, which reduces the effectiveness of emotional techniques.

Tricks of the trade

Here are some of the tricks of the trade that a negotiator should be aware of when contracting with professional services providers.

Travel, expenses and other additional costs

A budget holder agreed to pay for three specialist trainers to commute weekly (business class) from New York to London and rent an apartment in a smart part of London for six months. The travel and accommodation cost came to about the same as the total day rate costs. In general, the purchaser should look out for not just travel, but costs for telephone calls, photocopying, and so on. It might be considered a bit rich for a firm to charge for such extras when it is charging high day rates for a consultant, but some firms are not embarrassed to do so. Such expenses should be part of the initial negotiation and either disallowed or capped.

Billing hours ... and hours ... and hours

Kate (not her real name) is a partner at a top London law firm. She bills clients around 50 hours a week, which is impressive as she also has significant other responsibilities, including staff management, selling and client management. Back in the 1990s, New York firms started to enter the UK market. To many people's surprise, their hourly rates were slightly lower generally than those of the top London firms. Kate could not understand this, but one evening she met an old friend who had joined one of these ambitious and expanding American firms who said:

> It's simple. We're paying about 20% more than London rates to our staff, but the expectation is we all bill about 30% more hours per week. So the firm overall does just fine. I'm now billing clients for 80 hours a week.

Kate asked how that could be physically possible:

> Firstly, we do work really hard. The ethic is very powerful. But more critically, we bill everything. My clients get billed for my time in the shower and over breakfast in the morning. I'm thinking about their assignments, you see. And in the evening ... and at weekends. So I'm billing 12–14 hours a day Monday to Friday, then another 10–20 hours over the weekend.

Can anyone perform an intellectual job at a reasonable level for 80 hours a week? Or focus on a complex legal case while washing their hair? And were the clients aware that this was going on?

The billing process, which is also relevant to the management of the contract, should be part of the negotiation.

Time recording and definition of a "day"

Although a government department had negotiated a competitive set of day rates with a consulting firm for a major assignment, the cost was running well over budget. When the purchasing manager examined the invoices the reason became clear. The consulting firm was keeping detailed time sheets, then adding up the hours for the entire month for each consultant and dividing by 7.5, the hours in a standard working day. The result was defined as "days worked" and was then multiplied by the day rate to give the monthly billing amount.

A typical consultant who sat alongside the internal team from, say, 8.30–6 with 30 minutes for lunch (which most internal staff did as a matter of course) was working around 45 hours a week. Dividing that by 7.5 comes to six, so the department was charged the day rate times six each week, not the five that was expected. The costs were coming in around 20% higher than expected.

A brief and direct negotiation with the partner responsible for the assignment changed the basis for calculating "days worked". Any overtime would have to be authorised in advance, and would only be paid if the consultants were required to work at least two hours more than the standard day.

Promotions

Some law firms show surprisingly low day rates for partners on major framework agreements. But work with them and it becomes clear that almost everyone is a "partner". Few staff are charged at the lower rates for more junior staff. Similarly, in consulting, a promotion or two within a firm during a lengthy project can lead to the bill for a team of consultants rising considerably. This can be protected against in the contractual negotiations but needs watching when the assignment is under way.

Negotiation opportunities

As well as the tricks of the trade, a good negotiator should be aware of the opportunities that may present themselves. Charles Findlay (see page 155) talks about the value that can be gained from getting some free advice from partners. This will only work when a firm is or has the prospect of getting a significant amount of work, and it is worth exploring when it may be possible.

Professional services firms love certainty and volume commitment (discussed in Chapters 15 and 16). Where this can be offered, make sure a commensurate reduction against rate-card pricing is negotiated.

As well as an option to provide some free advice at the partners' discretion, some professional services firms have an internal fund to subsidise interesting or groundbreaking work that they can then use more widely. If an assignment falls into that category, try to negotiate a discount. A large insurance company paid £100,000 rather than around £500,000 for an assignment that the provider saw as an opportunity to enter an interesting market sector and a new area of technology implementation.

Other negotiable added value might come from training or skills transfer activities, or co-operation in joint ventures. Another angle is to consider what benefits can be offered to the supplier (aside from simply cash) that the supplier might trade in negotiation for benefit in return. For instance, offering to be a referee for other potential clients may have considerable value to the supplier. This could be a written reference or even agreeing to act as a reference site for visits by prospective customers. If the purchasing organisation has a recognisable, blue-chip name (whether public or private sector), there is a value to the supplier simply through association. Use that where possible.

As Darin Matthews explains below, even in a regulated government purchasing environment, well-developed negotiation skills and the ability to make the most of the opportunities that exist to negotiate make it more likely that the contracts entered into for professional services will result in better value for money.

Regional government of Portland, Oregon

"From cradle to grave" is how Darin Matthews, chief purchasing officer at Metro, the elected regional government of the Portland, Oregon, metropolitan area, describes the extent of his responsibilities. Everything in the purchasing process, from advertising contract opportunities to contract management and end-of-life disposal, comes under his remit across operations as diverse as Oregon Zoo and the city's cemeteries.

This means that Matthews's small team are responsible for third-party expenditure of around $100m a year. However, his influence on public purchasing in the United States goes further than that. He served as president of the National Institute for Governmental Purchasing in 2006 and now sits on the governing board of the Universal Purchasing Certification Council. He writes and speaks on purchasing topics, has contributed to textbooks on purchasing, has lectured at the University of Victoria, Rose State College and Cleveland State University, and teaches at Florida Atlantic University. Of the many changes Matthews has seen in purchasing over the past 20 years, the increased involvement of procurement departments in purchasing professional services is a notable one. He observes:

Looking across public procurement in the United States, it's only in the last decade that professional services has been seen as a key area for purchasing professionals and input. Even ten years ago, we would rarely be involved in the engagement of architects, consultants or lawyers. Much would have been done by the budget holder, or an estates/general services function, and purchasing would have been lucky just to see a copy of the final contract. Now it is expected that purchasing will be involved. So we must have the level of skill necessary to succeed in these categories.

He believes that a challenge for the profession, particularly in government purchasing, is to be able to shift thinking in an organisation "from the view that purchasing is here to help me write a bid specification, to the view that purchasing helps me to achieve my overall goals and I don't know how I'd manage without them". A more specific challenge is the seniority of people in the professional services firms that purchasing staff have to work with. Matthews explains:

My people are negotiating and working with very smart, senior people; they have to be able to cope with that. But we don't have the capacity to negotiate every contract. So a big part of my role is giving budget holders the tools and capability to carry out purchasing themselves. We enable, empower, delegate, train and provide oversight.

How can a small team make sure that happens across such a wide range of activities? Matthews says:

I constantly evaluate the skills of my team, not just how they negotiate or write a contract, but how they collaborate with colleagues, communicate effectively and run projects. People skills are at least as important as technical skills. I suspect purchasing people have always needed these skills, but perhaps it's just in the last few years we've realised this.

Professional services gives his people more scope than many categories in terms of the potential for real negotiation:

Procurement rules restrict us somewhat from full negotiation as the private sector would expect – but professional services contracts in particular are rarely tied down to every detail at tender stage. Even post tender, we often have to negotiate the detail around contract deliverables or exclusions, quality, payment mechanisms, changes in schedule and the consultants being proposed. Negotiation is critical.

Sustainable procurement in its widest sense (encompassing environmental, social and economic sustainability, see Chapter 20) is an important issue for Metro, which considers itself to be a leader in this field:

Even in professional services, we are looking at our suppliers' sustainability practices, for example at the effect on the local economy of using smaller firms. We recently awarded a major contract to a supplier who committed to recruiting staff from one of the most depressed areas in Oregon, and that did help the supplier in our evaluation.

Matthews has used framework arrangements with some success:

We will issue a request for qualification in legal services, for instance, and appoint between eight and ten providers to an approved list. We will then call off their services as required, reserving the right to run further competition between them if we think that is beneficial or necessary.

Contract management is also crucial to ensure that, wherever possible, contracts have clear deliverables and milestones and real value is delivered. Reporting requirements must be clear and focus on the deliverables, and much depends on having a clear definition of the scope of the work. "Helping the user to get that right is a key skill for my staff as far as I'm concerned," says Matthews.

Given his background and experience, it is not surprising that Matthews has strong views on how public organisations could improve performance. Some public bodies – including the State of Oregon – still use a process known as "qualification-based selection", which means that the assessment of suppliers is done purely on technical qualifications and capability without reference to price. Only when the preferred supplier is chosen is price "negotiated". Matthews argues:

Obviously, the public body is negotiating from a position of weakness at that point. Price should be a factor, not the only one of course, but I believe it must be drawn into the equation if we're going to deliver value for our taxpayers.

Delivering value will be doubly important in a future where public spending will be under unprecedented pressure:

Although the pricier firms may find life more difficult, headcount limits often mean more interim staff and temporary labour, all of which needs effective purchasing. So professional services is going to be an important spend category for the foreseeable future.

15 Understanding structures and costs

Tolstoy famously began *Anna Karenina* with the words: "Happy families are all alike; every unhappy family is unhappy in its own way."

The idea that the structures of organisations – families, businesses or government departments – are similar when they are functioning well, but evolve in different directions when they are not, provides a good starting point when thinking about how professional services firms are organised internally. The structure of a professional services firm drives its cost base and that, in turn, drives its fee rates. If they understand the structure and cost base, purchasers will have a good idea of how much room there is (or is not) to negotiate on price.

For Chicago-based procurement expert Jason Busch, a good understanding of how professional firms are structured is essential:

> The big spend decisions in these areas are made by end-users.
> Purchasing is often not involved, and where it dabbles it is more
> dangerous than no involvement. In my experience, if you beat
> up firms on day rate, the firms will get you back in other ways.
> You may find that less good people are put onto the project,
> or that it takes twice as long. It is vital to be able to segment
> the market and understand the nature of the resources being
> provided. For example, a bid may be cheaper because more of
> the work will be offshored to a low-cost location (something
> we've been seeing much more of since the start of the recession).
> The purchaser must understand that and look at things
> holistically. What, for instance, is the management cost to the
> client going to be, not just the hourly rate of the advisers? The
> best clients in the United States are aligning their advisers with
> the value they get from the work, through risk-reward or similar
> mechanisms.

The pyramid firm

The typical structure of a professional services firm is a pyramid. A small number of highly skilled people sit at the apex above descending layers of bright but decreasingly skilled people. The number of layers in the pyramid varies from firm to firm: some pride themselves on their flat organisations; others prefer a rigid chain of command. But the essential structure remains the same.

That sameness can be traced back to one influential book. David Maister was a British academic who taught at Harvard from 1979 to 1985, and his book, *Managing the Professional Service Firm*, was the culmination of many years' research with a wide variety of firms. He observed that professional services firms are distinctive for the high level of both customisation and client interaction involved in their work, which means they have to attract and retain highly skilled individuals. Like other companies, professional services firms compete on two fronts: in their client markets to win business, and in the labour market to recruit the best people. Maister remarks:

> *It is the need to balance the often conflicting demands and constraints imposed by these two markets that creates the special challenge of managing the professional service firm.*

At the heart of the pyramid structure are two features: leverage and utilisation.

Leveraging the people assets

The time of the senior people at the top of the pyramid is scarce and valuable. A firm that allows each senior person to spend all their time on one project cannot grow because the number of projects it can take on is limited by the number of hours senior people can work. This is why many niche firms, set up by senior and experienced people from other, bigger firms, find it so hard to grow. The only way to do so is to reduce the burden on the senior people by bringing in more junior staff to do some of the work. This allows the partners to spread their time across more projects. This is leverage: the extent to which the time of the people at the top of the pyramid can be levered by those further down. Of course, firms vary. A specialist legal practice may have five partners and ten associates because each assignment requires considerable partner input. By contrast, an IT consulting firm may have 20–50 junior consultants for every partner. Some of these differences are cultural (law firms have historically had lower ratios of junior to senior people, for instance), but the primary driver is the type of service offered. In short, the more standardised the service, the higher is the level of leverage. Thus a firm offering the same or a similar service requires less partner input, relying instead on a methodology that encapsulates what it does and training its junior staff to do the work of partners.

The long-term impact of increased leverage is lower prices. As a service becomes more familiar it becomes codified: clients want to know what they are buying and professional services firms need to know what they are supplying, so it is in everyone's interest to clarify what is involved. Over time, however, this becomes a process, even a series of check boxes, so fewer specialised skills are needed. As the level of expertise required falls, it becomes harder for professional services firms to differentiate themselves; clients see all firms offering the same service and start to choose on price. Lower margins mean that professional services firms cannot afford to place senior people on projects and a vicious circle ensues.

It should be easy to avoid this scenario by making sure that enough senior people's time is spent on any given project. This would not only differentiate a firm and prove to clients that this is a service worth paying over the odds for, but also ensure that the service evolves and that new ideas are injected into what might otherwise become too formulaic. But three forces work against this common-sense approach:

- **Business development.** Small professional services firms typically suffer from what the industry describes as the feast-or-famine problem. If the partners are wholly involved in working for clients, they have little or no time to spend on bringing in new business; as a result, the firm's performance swings wildly between being extremely busy (delivering the current project) and extremely quiet (finding the next project). The only way to resolve this is to free partners' time so they can continually develop the business, not just in fits and starts.
- **Career development.** As Maister points out, professional services firms compete in the labour market as much as in their client market. One of the most important ways to attract and retain the best people is to offer them challenging, varied work and a clear path to the top. A pyramid firm does this: because junior people are used to doing some of the work of more senior ones and because almost all projects require a mix of people at different levels, junior people have greater opportunities to develop their skills and further their careers than people in conventional line management roles. Limiting the amount of time junior people work with their senior colleagues also limits and slows down their career development.

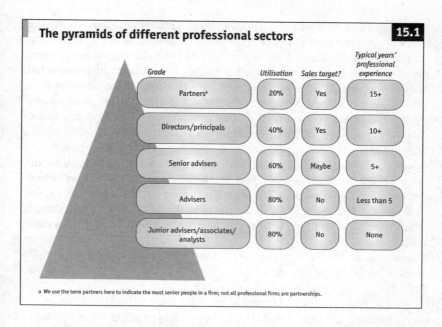

The pyramids of different professional sectors 15.1

Grade	Utilisation	Sales target?	Typical years' professional experience
Partners[a]	20%	Yes	15+
Directors/principals	40%	Yes	10+
Senior advisers	60%	Maybe	5+
Advisers	80%	No	Less than 5
Junior advisers/associates/analysts	80%	No	None

a We use the term partners here to indicate the most senior people in a firm; not all professional firms are partnerships.

▨ **Margins.** From a buying point of view, it is essential to understand that the people at the bottom of the pyramid are more profitable to use than those at the top. There is therefore no short-term economic incentive for professional services firms to reduce leverage.

Utilisation: keeping people busy

Utilisation is the clock that professional services firms keep time to. Every professional adviser knows their utilisation rate – the proportion of their time over a given period spent on chargeable, billable work for clients. Taking into account holidays, training, sickness and some degree of internal or business development work, the average utilisation rate for a professional services firm is around 65%. Lawyers generally measure utilisation in billable hours per week or per year worked: their target is 30–50 billable hours per person per week, a somewhat higher level than consultants.

Utilisation is important for two reasons: it dictates the structure and culture of a firm; and combined with leverage, it drives profitability.

Professional advisers usually have personal utilisation targets. Put simply, they have to keep themselves busy and they get promoted if they can keep their immediate colleagues busy. The higher they progress up the pyramid the lower their target utilisation rate will be, as this takes into account their spending more time developing the business and managing people, but it is rare for anyone to have no utilisation target. Even the most senior people will do some work with clients, partly because they enjoy it (it is why they joined the firm in the first place) and partly because status in a professional services firm is often a function of the quality of clients people work with: the more senior the people, the more high-profile are their clients.

Movement up the pyramid does not just depend on utilisation, but also on work sold, the quality of work delivered, experience (although this is primarily important in setting the entry point for someone joining a firm) and, increasingly, client satisfaction. Figure 15.1 is an illustration of how the levels and targets are typically set in one type of professional firm (a consultancy).

The more utilised a professional services firm is, the more profits it makes, as Table 15.1 illustrates:

- The first scenario is a conventional firm with 52 staff. Its partners have a high daily rate and because they are paid more and spend less time on chargeable work their contribution to the firm's gross profit is negative. The work done by junior staff, by contrast, is much more profitable because the staff are paid less and spend almost all their time on client work. The firm's overall utilisation rate is 67%, reasonably close to the industry average, enabling it to earn a gross profit (before overheads) of $3.5m on income of $6.6m.
- The second shows the same firm with a higher than average level of utilisation, an almost unsustainably high 79%. It has an income of $8.1m and a gross profit of $5m, 44% higher than in the first scenario.
- The third shows the firm with a much lower than average utilisation rate of 29%. Income is down to $2.9m and the firm is making a £246,000 loss even before overheads.

Professional services firms have traditionally kept their fees close to their chest, and some firms still have "run rates" – the amount they charge per month for a given team – rather than a breakdown of individuals' fees or time. However, buyers should insist that a firm is clear not only about the rate charged for each person but also the amount of time that will be committed to a project.

Table 15.1 **The pyramid structure of a typical consulting firm**

	No. of staff	Daily rate ($)	Utilisation rate (%)	Income ($'000)	Costs ($'000)	Gross profit ($'000)	Gross profit (%)
Conventional scenario							
Partner	2	3,000	30	396	500	104	−26
Director/principal	5	1,500	50	825	600	225	27
Senior adviser	10	1,000	70	1,540	800	740	48
Adviser	15	800	70	1,848	750	1,098	59
Junior adviser/ associate/analyst	20	650	70	2,002	500	1,502	75
Average		1,390	67	127	61	67	52
Total				6,611	3,150	3,461	52
Super profits							
Partner	2	3,000	50	660	500	160	24
Director/principal	5	1,500	80	1,320	600	720	55
Senior adviser	10	1,000	80	1.760	800	960	55
Adviser	15	800	80	2,112	750	1,362	64
Junior adviser/ associate/analyst	20	650	80	2,288	500	1,788	78
Average		1,390	79	157	61	96	61
Total				8,140	3,150	4,990	61
Super losses							
Partner	2	3,000	20	264	500	236	−89
Director/principal	5	1,500	20	330	600	270	−82
Senior adviser	10	1,000	30	660	800	140	−21
Adviser	15	800	30	792	750	42	5
Junior adviser/ associate/analyst	20	650	30	858	500	358	42
Average		1,390	29	56	61	5	−8
Total				2,904	3,150	246	−8

Reputation and plush offices notwithstanding, most professional services firms have experienced substantial increases in costs since 2000. Fierce competition for good people (temporarily masked by the global economic downturn) has pushed salaries up. Globalisation has required an investment in overseas offices and technology that would have been unimaginable 20 years ago. Failed projects and more litigious clients have pushed professional indemnity insurance rates up, sometimes hugely. Research by the UK Management Consultancies Association in 2007 suggests that the average pre-tax net profit for a consulting firm is a mere 7%. However, in many partnerships – whether law, audit or consulting firms – financial performance is usually expressed in terms of a profit-per-partner.

Other organisational models

As a result of shortcomings in the pyramid organisational structure, a number of different structures have been tried, most of which are still in their infancy.

One common criticism of professional services firms is that what you see at the sales pitch is not what you get in practice. A senior, highly experienced partner may turn up for the presentation that wins the work, but may rarely be involved in the project, the work being done instead by underlings. This does not mean the quality of work is poor; it is often extremely good. The point is whether it could have been better: the client thinks it is buying the senior person's time, only to be disappointed when it discovers that the person is committed to working on several projects at once. Leverage results in unhappy clients. It is why niche consultancies, staffed only with senior people, keep bubbling up to exploit opportunities.

A problem with the pyramid structure is that small changes in leverage and utilisation have a significant impact on a firm's profitability. This means it is continually struggling to recruit sufficient people to meet demand while simultaneously ensuring that it does not have too many "on the bench".

Some firms believe that the pyramid structure is not suited to the large-scale, global enterprises that dominate the professional services sector. Most want a model that is easier to adapt to changing demands; some also want to provide clients with the senior input they are typically looking for; all want to reduce their costs.

One option is to employ fewer full-time staff, replacing them with temporary staff, subcontractors or "associates". This has the advantage of being more flexible: temporary staff can be used to fill short-term spikes in demand without any long-term commitment for a firm. However, there are disadvantages: subcontractors may be less loyal and it is harder for a firm to control the quality of the work done. To get round these problems, virtual firms have emerged which employ only a small number of people whose role is to grow and manage the business; all the project work is done by freelance advisers. Gerson Lehrman, based in the United States, is essentially a sophisticated database of experts. Some may be working independently, retired or even employed by a firm, but all are available to work for clients looking for specialised expertise, such as private equity firms that need advice on an acquisition. Eden McCallum is a UK-based strategy consulting firm. Most of the people who work on its projects have worked at one of the big brand-name strategy firms but now want to work more flexibly. With around 500 associates on its books and a turnover of around £7m, Eden McCallum employs fewer than 30 people.

Another option has been to form alliances or joint ventures with other professional services firms. Thus two firms specialising in different fields can work together on a specific project or even develop a common service in a growing market. Such ventures range from an informal agreement to co-operate on a single piece of work to a long-term formal joint venture. Although fine in theory, such collaborations often fail in practice over, for example, arguments about who "owns" the clients. Where they succeed it is usually because the firms have a clear and equitable view of what each of them contributes; and they may be helped by a growing market in which there is plenty of space for each firm to win new work.

Ownership structure is a factor in all models of professional services firms, which historically were partnerships. The pyramid model relies on the expertise and business development skill of the people at its apex, who are the owners of the business and who determine its direction. Partnership structures have other advantages, principally that they are not forced to reveal their results and are not subject to the treadmill of quarterly reporting that large publicly listed corporations have to live with, making it easier for them to take on projects where the return may be spread over many years.

So why have so many partnerships converted themselves into public corporations? As is so often the case, it is to do with money. One of the weaknesses of a partnership structure is that it has relatively limited cash reserves (the money is taken out by the partners annually, although on the understanding that they may be asked to put money in if the business requires it). Many partnerships went public because they had outgrown the pyramid structure. The partner/consultant ratio of an IT services company may be 1:100, compared with 1:10 in a more traditional firm. In this environment, partnership-based decision-making becomes almost impossible. Individual partners become too powerful and construct their own mini-businesses, sometimes at the expense of their colleagues. Partners try to hold onto their earnings, thus depriving the business of the investment it requires. Everyone puts their interests first, so agreeing collective priorities is complicated. Often chaos reigns.

16 Payment and commercial models

Daryl Atkinson, director of marketing at Charles Russell, an international law firm with offices in London, Geneva and the Middle East, says:

> We think of our pricing strategy as reflecting three types of engagement. The first we call the "haircut": the client wants to know what it costs in advance and that's not unreasonable. We should be able to work out our costs accurately and offer a fixed price – like buying a haircut. The second is the "broken arm": the client needs it fixed pretty urgently, and the work is fairly predictable, but with some issues and uncertainties that make it harder to predict precisely our effort and costs. Here, we can estimate fees with some accuracy but we require a bit more flexibility in the way we price. Finally, there is the "heart attack": the client doesn't care too much what it costs, but just needs us to do whatever is necessary to get it sorted. Pricing reflects that need: our pricing approaches have to be very different for each of these types of work.

Procurement expert Jason Busch says:

> Not all purchasing people have the commercial "savvy" to influence top management and "sell" their desired approach. Good market knowledge and external benchmarks help. If a purchasing manager can quote a benchmarked rate for similar services, then he can convince a budget holder that a quote is unreasonable. Purchasing can gain credibility by talking about value rather than price, and by being smart on ideas to measure value and capture risk reduction.

The cost structure of a professional services firm goes a long way to explaining the basis on which most are charged for professional help. Of the three methods used, time and materials and fixed price are straightforward, and the third, performance related payments based on sharing risks and rewards, is less so.

Time and materials

Professional services firms have traditionally based their charges on the time spent and costs incurred by the people who work for them. The more senior and experienced a person, the more is charged for their time.

One of the advantages of charging for time spent is transparency, as time sheets will be available to check invoices. However, two recent changes, often introduced by procurement teams, have inadvertently eroded this.

First, all professional services firms would, at least until recently, have charged their expenses separately. However, clients, wise to the risk that expenses are hard to budget for, now often ask for expenses to be included in the hourly or daily rate. This makes administration and budgeting easier, but it is not cost-effective in the long run because the professional services firm will have to increase its fees to allow for expenses and to cover the risk of unexpected expenses being incurred.

The second change is the emergence of "blended" rates. In theory, it should be easy for someone to compare the rates quoted by several professional services firms for the same piece of work, but different grading structures make this hard to do. One firm's senior consultant is another's programme manager; one firm's director is another firm's partner. The proportion of work done by each grade may also vary. One firm may use a couple of senior people for two days a week; another may use one senior person for slightly longer but supported by two full-time junior staff. Similar work may be done by two people of the same grade but in different locations, each with a different charge-out rate: the person based in New York is more expensive than the one based in India.

Blended rates have been introduced to deal with these variations. Rather than submitting different rates for different people or grades, professional services firms have been asked to provide a single average rate. This approach makes like-for-like comparisons easier but has several drawbacks. It makes professional fees less, not more, transparent. What really goes into a "blended" mix? This takes time and materials back to an even older model, still used by some strategy firms, of "run-rate" – the fee per month for all the staff involved in a project. It creates an incentive for the professional services firm to use as cheap a mix of people as possible, thus clawing back some of the margin lost in the combined rate. It also makes it harder for small firms to compete because they typically employ a greater proportion of senior people and have a higher average rate than a large firm employing many juniors. So in asking for blended rates there is the risk of reducing competition.

Two underlying flaws with payment based on time and materials are that it does not give the professional services firm an incentive to work efficiently, and it is hard for clients to control and contain the budget. Many complain that it feels as though they have a meter running and that the firms they work with are constantly looking for opportunities to bring in more people or stay for longer. However, pricing in isolation is never a panacea. It is tempting to assume that because time and materials is the traditional mode of payment, it is old-fashioned and wrong. But if there is uncertainty about the scale and scope of an assignment, which is often the case in professional services, it may make sense to pay for help as it is needed. This payment method can also be a sign of trust between the client and the professional services firm; they may have worked together before and the client may see no reason to offer further incentives.

Fixed price

The element of customisation in most professional services work is the reason fixed-price contracts are not more widely used across the industry. The more standardised the service (tax compliance, some legal and IT services), the more likely the charge for it will be fixed; the more the scope and content of a project are ambiguous and uncertain, the less willing a supplier will be to fix the price.

The price of a fixed-price contract can be arrived at in two ways:

- ◪ Input (cost-plus) pricing. The supplier works out how much time and what kind of resources it is likely to need on a project, then adds to that an element of contingency and the margin it would expect to make.
- ◪ Output (value) pricing. The supplier looks at what the work is worth to the client, irrespective of the time involved.

There is a story which explains the difference between the two approaches. A newspaper's only printing press breaks down. Unable to print, the company can earn no money. Its own engineers fail to fix the problem so the company calls in an expert. He arrives, takes a look, tightens a tiny screw and the press starts working. The relieved publisher thanks the expert and asks him to send his bill only to get a shock when he receives it. "How can you charge us $25,000 for five minutes' work?" he rages. "Send me an itemised bill." When it arrives, the bill states simply: "For five minutes' work fixing the printing press, $5; for knowing how to fix the printing press, $24,995.".

In theory, fixed-price contracts provide reassurance to the client that there will be no surprises about the cost of a project and give an incentive to the supplier to do the work as cost effectively as possible.

In practice, fixed-price contracts can end up being just as problematic as ones based on time and materials. Suppliers in danger of exceeding their budgets may cut corners or argue that specific requests are beyond the scope originally agreed and therefore should be charged extra for.

Risk-reward

A risk-reward basis for charging can involve the following:

- **Carrot or stick.** The focus ranges from the negative ("If you do not achieve X, we will not pay you Y") to the positive ("If you achieve X, we will pay you Y").
- **Standard fee or bonus.** Meeting a target may simply entitle a professional services firm either to a "normal" fee, typically calculated on a time and materials basis, or to some type of bonus.
- **All or part.** Many professional service firms are willing to invoice for their costs during the project, making the final, say, 20% of their fee dependent on how satisfactory the outcome is. However, in some cases firms are prepared to make their fees entirely dependent on a successful outcome, as when lawyers work on a no-win, no-fee basis.

Generalist firms, working on projects where the scope is uncertain or ambiguous and which require considerable interaction with a client's own staff, do very little, if any, risk-reward work. Specialists in a particular field, where projects are more likely to be measurable and self-contained, are more likely to work on a risk-reward basis. But they are in a minority for a variety of reasons.

Clients often feel uncomfortable agreeing to too large a reward, in part because of the common perception that a risk-reward arrangement is primarily concerned with transferring risk, rather than rewarding good performance. In the public sector, where less than 5% of expenditure on professional services is on a risk-reward basis compared with around twice that in the private sector, scale, the complexity of stakeholder management and procurement rules make risk-reward less feasible. But the main constraint is budgets. Managers have a specific budget and it is difficult for them to go back to ask for more "reward" money, even though the professional services firm might have generated extra savings.

Where risk-reward is used, it may sometimes be adopted for the wrong reasons. A client who is uncertain about the value the advisers will add may opt for this approach, not to ensure a firm's commitment to a specific goal, but to avoid paying for a project that might fail. (If that were the case, a better approach would be to increase the probability of success or cancel the project.) Equally, where a client is confident the project will have a successful outcome, there is little incentive to create a bonus structure that rewards the professional services firm for doing no more than it would in any case. One of the ironies of risk-reward deals is that they are more likely to be used where the chances of success are low. Moreover, although risk-reward deals are touted as a means of aligning the objectives of customers and suppliers, there is a risk that they will do the opposite. Risk-reward is often a tool of inexperienced buyers who think they will save money and are not sure the project will be successful.

Risk-reward arrangements can be unduly expensive, especially if the scope is not clear at the outset. They can also be problematic because it is difficult and often time-consuming to measure the benefits, and they can encourage the wrong behaviour. For example, if the payment of a team of consultants implementing an IT system depends on ensuring it goes live on a specific date, they are more likely to cut corners to meet that deadline. They will act in their own interest, not that of their clients.

Risk-reward arrangements work best in large-scale projects, which are clearly defined in terms of scope, inputs and the desired outcome and where the outputs will be measurable. And they will only work where the client–supplier relationship is collaborative; if it is adversarial, they will only add to the tension between the parties involved.

Performance-related fees

In all his time managing global brands, Neil Punwani can recall only one creative agency offering to stake a substantial part of their base fee on a performance-related basis:

> They were a small, innovative agency pitching for a $1m-plus contract against many better-known names. Instead of quoting a single fee, as the bigger agencies did, they suggested that we pay them in instalments, one-third up front, one-third on success of initial test results (together these would cover their costs) and one-third (effectively, their profit element) if they achieved the objectives we set for market success. We were happy with their approach,

so were quite open to the idea. But then the lawyers stepped in. What metrics should we use to gauge satisfaction? Who should do the measuring? What if the agency scored well in some areas and not others? What if our company changed direction and targets were not met due to internal decisions? What would happen if the agency didn't agree with our assessment, or we didn't agree with theirs? The whole thing was starting to feel like a legal game.

To pre-empt potential deadlock, the matter was resolved by putting into the contract a statement to the effect that the decision over whether the last third of the fees would be paid would be based ultimately on the discretion of Punwani and his colleagues.

In the end it came down to a handshake with their CEO. The lawyers couldn't believe it, that the agency would be willing to do this, but both sides accepted that it came down to judgment. In the end, we paid the majority of the total fee but not all of it: the agency didn't achieve every objective but we felt they'd worked well and done much of what we'd asked them to. The arrangement worked because we trusted each other as individuals. I can see why agencies and clients are nervous about paying for professional services on this basis – but sometimes the most critical element in thinking creatively about performance and remuneration is personal relationships and trust.

Open book

Any approach to pricing relies on transparency if it is not to become a bone of contention between professional services firms and their clients, so it is increasingly common for contracts and payment approaches to include open book arrangements.

Open book gives the purchaser the right to inspect the provider's records to check that what the provider is charging is supported by hard evidence. The purchaser may check on the amount of effort expended by the provider, pay rates or other costs that the provider claims to have incurred in carrying out the contract.

Although it can be useful, it does rely on the accuracy and veracity of the providers' records; and checking on costs and effort does not of course guarantee that the purchaser has received good value for money, or the output or deliverables required. It does, though, give the purchaser some basic protection against obvious provider overcharging or even fraud.

Cutting the bill

Three driving forces have been behind reductions in fees that have been seen in professional services:

- Each successive economic downturn appears to have increased the willingness of professional services firms to discount in the short term to see off the competition, fearful that if they do not, they risk opening the door to new entrants at a time when they should be consolidating existing relationships with long-standing clients.
- Moves towards sharing information on suppliers, especially in the public sector, is leading to greater and more widespread transparency.
- The standardisation (or commoditisation) of some professional services makes it harder for firms to differentiate their offerings. Because these services all look the same, clients feel spoilt for choice, which encourages a focus on low price. Indeed, one of the ironies of professional services is that, for all the talk of maintaining fee rates, it is often the firms themselves that volunteer discounts. Like their clients, they are not always sure of the value they add.

But in seeking a cut in the bill, care needs to be taken to ensure that reduced fees do not simply reflect reduced quality – for example, through the use of more junior staff or a simpler, more standardised process.

Another consideration is the timing of payments – an important factor with long-term contracts, such as big implementation projects that are spread over several years and "back-loaded" so that the fees paid to the supplier are higher in later years. Penalties for early termination of the contract provide compensation should suppliers be deprived of the more lucrative years of income. But most professional services contracts are shorter, so there is less opportunity for back-loading.

Increasingly, however, organisations are looking to spread their payments for professional services and, where possible, match payments against savings resulting from the services. Consulting firms, for example, talk of clients who have offered to pay more for their services, provided payment can be deferred by a year, by which time the savings resulting from the work will have come through.

Negotiating for late payment can be worth doing, but if a client ends up paying more than it would otherwise, it is, in effect, borrowing from the supplier and should only do so if it makes good business sense.

Ron Jarman of Universal Music and buyingTeam explains below how he uses risk/reward payment mechanisms and when it is not appropriate to do so. He says that risk must be allocated properly when determining the most appropriate contractual and payment structure.

Purchaser or consultant?

Ron Jarman has an unusual role. Having served as global head of indirect purchasing at Diageo and global head of sourcing at Reuters, he is now chief procurement officer at Universal Music Group International. At the same time he is a consultant, working for buyingTeam, a leading procurement consulting and outsourcing service provider, under whose auspices he is now working at Universal Music. Jarman explains:

I'm gamekeeper and poacher rolled into one. I'm a provider of professional services to Universal, but my team here manages the purchase of professional services, including consulting and legal, for Universal.

The team of 25 people look after some $1 billion in annual expenditure, everything from IT and facilities to make-up artists and recording studios:

That means we can't take the traditional purchasing approach to everything we do – we have to be flexible and creative ourselves.

Jarman's career means he has seen and put into practice different approaches to purchasing at several blue-chip organisations, but professional services has always been one of the most difficult aspects of his work. In particular, relationships play a more crucial role than in other spending areas; his team has to work with people who are far more senior than they are, sometimes board directors, many of whom know the partners in the consulting, legal or audit firm they want to work with. Suppliers, too, know who makes the decisions, so purchasing staff can easily be bypassed, especially if they are perceived to be getting in the way. Jarman says:

We can't afford to act as a bottleneck. The role of my team is to co-ordinate and facilitate contact, not to stop it.

It is also important to achieve what Gartner, a research company, calls "team equivalence": purchasing staff must be credible to the people they deal with in professional services firms and to internal stakeholders, and investment in purchasing should match that made on the provider side. It is as much about attitude and approach as about experience and skills because the key is what Jarman calls "business-led demand management", helping the business use professional advisers appropriately, speaking softly rather than carrying a big stick:

It is who you use, when you use them and how you use them. Getting a lower day rate is well down my list of priorities in terms of delivering value.

Experience has taught Jarman the importance of developing a well-thought-out plan for each category (and subcategory), not just negotiating lower rate-card prices. Different categories may need different approaches. Setting up and running a panel of legal services providers for routine transactions can be handled as a standard operational purchasing task. Audit is another reasonably standard service:

But at the other end of the spectrum, engaging a consulting firm for some sensitive, board-level advice on a merger or acquisition is a very different game.

This means that segmentation is crucial: even within a category such as legal services, Jarman will differentiate between work that can be done out of London or even offshored, and that which really needs face-to-face input from "magic circle" firms.

Price helps to ensure that providers deliver once they are engaged. Jarman rightly expects a lot from providers of expensive services. Deliverables must be clear, and providing incentives is crucial:

But you have to recognise that some assignments just don't lend themselves to a risk-reward approach. Where the nature of the work allows it, I would look for a fixed-price deal which included an element of income at risk for the supplier. Risk has to be positioned with whoever is best placed to manage it, so you have to be careful.

Jarman has two main concerns. First, too large a penalty can lead to dysfunctional behaviour, perhaps a provider walking away from an assignment or looking for a legal way out. Second, success depends on the nature of the firm: a large professional services firm can afford to put a reasonable amount of income at risk, but it may not be reasonable to ask a small firm to do the same:

If I had to generalise, I would often look to around plus or minus 20% of a "normal" day rate as enough to motivate without going too far. But where we've used consultants implanted as part of my team, we've aligned interests by giving them the same percentage bonus that staff could achieve for high performance. I'm happy for suppliers to make money above their base rate, as long as it's not too much.

Jarman and his team also look at the percentage of partner billing to make sure it is not out of line. They also try to avoid duplication of work – different bits of the organisation paying different advisers to do the same piece of work – both of which he has found to yield substantial savings:

But that means you really have to know what's going on in your own organisation. I've even in the past found expensive projects still running, when the board had explicitly closed them down months before.

He has had his share of bad experiences too:

In one of the organisations I worked for, the finance department hired a professional services firm to advise them on their payables strategy. The resulting advice wasn't rocket science – to extend payment terms in countries where we were paying faster than the local practice – but they charged us a lot for that piece of stunningly obvious advice. To add insult to injury, they wouldn't accept the extended terms that they themselves had recommended. Firms such as these probably have more smart people working for them than any other businesses in the world, but intelligence often goes with arrogance.

However, Jarman is the first to recognise that pricing only gets you so far and has therefore encouraged his team to avoid the type of adversarial relationship so often found between purchasing departments and professional services firms. He points out that managers often find it easy to praise staff and hard to criticise; with providers, the reverse is often true. "Just praising a provider for good work can be highly motivating," he points out.

17 The contract

A good contract defines responsibilities clearly, is easy to understand, and is reasonable and balanced in the eyes of both parties. As such, it sets the scene for a relationship that may not require much contractual argument.

But the converse is not necessarily true. The fact that the buyer is not constantly referring back to the contract may indicate that they have little ability to use or even understand it, or the contract may be so weak that it offers no real value or protection. In extreme cases, there may not even be a contract or no one may know where to find it. "We never consult the contract" is a polite way of saying "We lack the skills to manage the contract or supplier and just accept whatever the supplier tells us". A poor contract will lead in all likelihood either to one party being exploited, or to a constant round of contractual referrals and disputes.

Getting the contract right is crucial. If it is never referred to that is fine, but making it a low priority because it will not be referred to is to confuse cause and effect.

The core of the contract

At the heart of the contract are a description of what the supplier is agreeing to do and the nature of the payment it will receive for that work. In a professional services contract, the details will depend on the nature of the agreement. The contract will vary considerably between, for instance, a low value call-off order where a framework contract is already in place, a detailed requirement for a fixed-price deliverable, or a time and materials contract for a defined project. But there are some common features relating to the work and the payment for it. Work-related details include:

- What – a clear description of the deliverables, outputs or results to which the supplier is committing, or the inputs (usually the people) if it is a contract without clear deliverables.
- When – the timing of delivery.
- How – an explanation of how it will be delivered and what the outputs will look like (a written report, a piece of software).

Payment-related details include:

◻ How much will be paid and in what units (for example, daily or hourly rate, monthly stage payments).

◻ When payments will be made (for example, timing of interim or stage payments).

◻ Conditions for payment (for example, success-related fees).

Much of the rest of the contract relates to "what if" elements of the assignment. What if one party goes out of business? What if there is a breach of security, or the supplier does not perform, or the buyer does not pay? A good contract describes how such matters are to be addressed or corrected so that both parties know what to expect.

What a good contract should look like

The contract should be appropriate to the scale and risk of the assignment. A few hours of work from a lawyer may not require more than an e-mail confirming an hourly rate and a brief description of the output required; even if the advice is important, it may not be worth producing a formal contract. This is where frameworks and preferred supplier lists can be useful. The buying organisation and the provider have the protection of a framework with some agreed terms and conditions, which then apply even in the case of small assignments.

Most importantly, the contract should capture and reflect the agreement between the parties. This may sound obvious, but it is surprising how often it is not the case. For instance, both parties may talk about the need for collaborative relationships in a big consulting assignment. But once the lawyers have got hold of it, the contract can turn into a series of potential crimes and punishments, full of penalties, get-out clauses and aggressive positioning by one or both parties.

There are many standard contracts available, tailored for local legislation, some of which are specifically applicable to professional services. Most should contain the elements listed above as the core of the contract. However, it is worth noting the approach taken by Tim Ussher (see page 85). He developed a set of terms and conditions specifically for consulting services that combined elements from existing contracts, including suppliers' standard contracts, to ensure the final contract fully met Virgin Media's needs.

The rest of this chapter focuses on some of the details that are most likely to be important or difficult when negotiating a professional services contract.

The main contract terms

The sections and specific clauses described below are often useful in a standard professional services contract.

General terms

- Definition of the initial contract period.
- Any potential contract extension periods. It is usually advisable to include at least the potential for contract extension if it is needed.
- Conflict of interest issues. These can be important professional services; for instance, a client may wish to ensure a consultant is not working simultaneously for a competitor firm, or advising on an acquisition where the consultant has a stake in the firms involved.

Services to be supplied

Clauses concerning the delivery of the services can be included here. A detailed specification or description of services may also be included but this is usually attached as a schedule.

- Commitment to supply the services.
- Provision and removal of equipment. This may be relevant, for example, in terms of providing IT equipment for consultants working on the client's site.
- Personnel. This can be important if the purchasing organisation wants to make sure the provider uses certain individuals on the project.
- Right to refuse access or remove from the contract. This can give the client the right to decide which individuals from the provider's firm work on the assignment.
- Offers of employment. A common protection for both parties, this covers an agreement that the parties will not poach each other's staff (at least for a defined period).

Payment, contract price and tax

- Contract prices. Details may be attached as a schedule in which case this clause will make reference to that.
- Payment. This may be merely basic invoicing details and payment terms, or it may include more complex payment mechanisms.
- Taxes. Taxes payable with identified responsibility, for example liability for employment taxes in the case of interim staff.

- Recovery of sums due. This gives the customer the right to withhold payment for penalties and so on.
- Price adjustment if contract period extended. The basis for changes in pricing if this occurs (or the details may be part of a schedule).

Statutory obligations and regulations

These relate to the national law that will apply to the contract. For example:

- Prevention of corruption and fraud.
- Discrimination (sexual, religious, racial, and so on).
- Environmental requirements.
- Health and safety.
- Definition of which national law governs the contract.

Protection of information

Clauses under this heading will depend on the nature of the work. At one end of the scale is a consulting study for a national government concerning defence or security precautions; at the other is a quick piece of advice on property law. Security and confidentiality have become increasingly important as electronic communication and fears of terrorism have increased, and they are particularly important in the public sector, where there have been some well-publicised incidents involving professionals services firms. According to *The Register* in 2007, US military personnel were affected by the loss of data from a service provider. SAIC, a support services contractor, acknowledged that more than 500,000 serving military members could be at risk of identity theft after it failed to adequately protect and transfer data (unencrypted and across the internet). Areas covered may include the following:

- Legal requirements.
- How confidential information must be handled and any particular precautions the customer wishes the supplier to take.
- Freedom of information.
- Handling publicity or media enquiries.
- General security provisions.
- Right of the client to audit the provider.
- Intellectual property rights (this is a critical issue for many professional services assignments; see page 183 for more details).

Control of the contract

Clauses under this heading relate to contract performance and the actions that can be taken if performance is unsatisfactory.

- Monitoring of contract performance. This may include how contract management will be structured and reports to be produced by the provider.
- Transfer and subcontracting. The rights of either or both parties to subcontract or assign the contract to another organisation. The purchaser may want to make sure that the provider cannot subcontract if it has been engaged for its specific skills. The purchaser will generally want the right to assign, particularly for a longer-term contract where an organisation may change during the period of the contract (for example, through merger or acquisition).
- Variation. The rights of either party to vary the contract and how that might happen.
- Remedies in the event of inadequate performance. Costs and methods of putting right failures by the provider.
- Extension of initial contract period.

Liabilities

- Liability, insurance and indemnity. A range of general liabilities can be described, along with the insurance the provider is required to have in place.
- Professional indemnity. It is important that providers have appropriate insurance. However, the purchaser should be aware that demands for excessive levels of insurance will add to providers' costs and will squeeze smaller suppliers out of the market
- Warranties and representations. Any relevant underlying matters or facts as they are presented in the contract.

Default, disruption and termination

These clauses explain what will happen if something goes wrong during the assignment or contract period.

- Termination provisions. The actions the purchaser can take if the provider becomes insolvent, has a change of management or financial control, or defaults. This may also include the consequences, such as handling of outstanding payments.
- Disruption. What should happen if the contract is disrupted.

◼ Recovery upon termination. The requirement for the provider to return material or property to the customer when the contract terminates.
◼ *Force majeure.* What events are allowable under this clause, such as natural disasters, strikes or other civil disturbances.
◼ Dispute resolution. Arbitration and other forms of alternative dispute resolution (ADR) can be useful as a means of avoiding expensive legal action where a dispute cannot be resolved through discussion between the parties.

Schedules

Schedules can contain a range of documents describing how the assignment is to be carried out. For a major consulting assignment, for instance, there may be a list of all the consultants who are to work on it. Some examples of schedules are as follows:

◼ Specification. Details of how the work is to be done, deliverables or outputs.
◼ Pricing. Details of daily rates or other fees and payments.
◼ Monitoring/contract management schedule. How the assignment will be monitored or managed.
◼ Staff. Who is going to work on the assignment.
◼ Commercially sensitive information. What information must be treated with particular care.

Intellectual property

This is a crucial aspect of many professional services contracts. It is reasonable for the purchaser to own the rights to any intellectual property (IP) created by the provider when under contract – the purchaser may want to adapt it or use it as a basis for products that may be marketed. Physical materials – reports, presentations, software and so on – should also be delivered to and owned by the client. However, intellectual property created by consultants will often depend on other pre-existing rights, which may be owned either by the consulting firm or by third parties. In many cases, a consulting firm will be using IP it has developed over the years, and there is no question of transferring all rights to it. In such cases, the purchaser should make sure it can use the outputs of the assignment freely, and this can be covered in the contract.

It is not unusual for clients to pay for consultants to develop training material and then find they have to use those consultants to deliver the training. A reasonable compromise may be for clients to negotiate a perpetual licence to use IP that has not been developed purely for them but, for instance, not to resell or transfer it. In the case of third-party IP ownership, a consultant may, as part of an assignment, create a software program that depends on pre-existing software components. The rights to that software will not be transferred to the client, and the contract will need to cover the client's rights to use the pre-existing IP (without penalty) alongside the new rights.

Consultants will often seek to retain joint ownership of intellectual property, or at least the right to use it themselves in their future work. This is a matter for discussion and negotiation, and it is often reasonable to allow the consultant to do this. But if a consultant is developing something that gives real competitive advantage to the client, it may not be sensible to let the consultant take the IP and sell it to the competition. Contractual clauses can prevent this, or put a time limit on usage (for example, the client has exclusivity for a year after the assignment), or restrict use of the IP in certain market sectors.

PART 6
MANAGING THE SERVICE PROVIDER

The purchasing role should not stop when the contract is signed: skilful management of professional firms as they deliver their services is critical to getting good value for money, as well as the desired outcome. Indeed, more value can often be generated through effective supplier management than during the procurement process itself.

Not all services or suppliers are equal, however. The appropriate level of contract management should be determined by identifying and quantifying the risks and potential opportunities involved. Some professional services firms, those whose work is essential to the success of the purchasing organisation, will be "strategic partners". Most others will have an operational or just a tactical role. Clearly, there is no point investing resources in managing firms that work on one relatively unimportant project per year. By contrast, ensuring a regular exchange of information and putting in place a programme through which knowledge from the professional firm is systematically transferred to end-users can yield substantial dividends.

18 Contract and performance management

Procurement expert Jason Busch says:

> The best clients are getting into real vendor management,
> developing 360-degree scorecards for instance. But at the other
> extreme, we see organisations which don't bother to check
> advisers' billing, despite the fact that many professional services
> firms don't have very sophisticated billing systems, so checking is
> often necessary.

In all but the simplest professional services projects, skilful management of the contract and the supplier through to delivery is crucial in getting good value for money and the desired performance and outcome; it can also help overcome problems that arise when a contract is not well formulated. The converse is equally true: poor contract management increases the chances of the outcome being unsatisfactory.

Figure 18.1 reflects the views of senior purchasing managers on

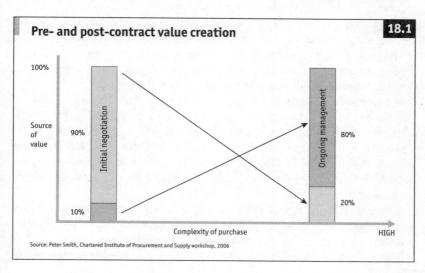

Pre- and post-contract value creation · 18.1

Source of value · Initial negotiation · Ongoing management · Complexity of purchase · HIGH · 100% · 90% · 10% · 80% · 20%

Source: Peter Smith, Chartered Institute of Procurement and Supply workshop, 2006

the activities that generate value in procurement contracts. For simple contracts, the initial negotiation determines the greatest amount of the value gained. For complex contracts, including those for professional services, up to 80% of the overall value created is dependent on good contract post-management. In short, the more complex the project the more the value derived depends on how well the contract and the supplier are managed.

The purpose of contract management

The core purpose of contract management is to make sure that the supplier delivers what has been agreed as defined by the contract.

With goods, a simple inspection may be enough to determine whether a supplier has met its contractual obligations. With a complex service, such as a long-term global consulting project, it is much more difficult to do so. Making sure that deliverables (which may be intangible) are produced as contracted, that payment mechanisms work effectively, that risks are well managed, and that the relationship between the consulting firm (the supplier) and the buying organisation is strong are all important and often demanding tasks that depend on effective contract and supplier management.

Assessing appropriate levels of contract management

Each contract and supplier needs to be assessed in terms of what post-contract activities are necessary and appropriate; these will largely depend on the complexity and timescale of the project.

The assessment should take into account the inherent risk, as that partly defines the potential benefit, and the potential value that can be derived above that defined in the contract. If there is no inherent risk, and no opportunities for additional value, there is no justification for more than basic contract management. This is true even if the contract value is large. The process depends on judgment but can be supported by a cost (effort)/benefit analysis of the activities that could be undertaken. But it would require certainty that the provider would deliver the services required, at the cost and time agreed. The other justification for contract management effort is the potential for additional value that could be obtained from the supplier – through, for example, reduced costs, improved service levels or additional innovation.

The analysis of risk and value should also help determine the contract management activities that should be undertaken. For example, a small contract for a simple piece of work should require only minimal supplier relationship and risk management. But if there is a significant risk of the

Table 18.1 **A contract management framework**

Underpinning essentials	Governance and administration
	People
Core management	Performance
	Relationship (operational)
	Payment
Development	Contract change and development
	Supplier development
	Supplier relationship management (see Chapter 19)
	Market management (see Chapter 19)

supplier failing to deliver something important, regardless of the pure monetary value of the contract, it could justify careful management of performance, risk, payment and relationships.

Identifying and quantifying risk and value opportunities

The different types of risk to consider include the following:

- **Failure to deliver the service as required.** This is a risk in contracts where the supplier fails to deliver, or the requirement was not clearly defined or specified. It is prevalent in areas such as outsourced service provision or IT services, but it could arise from failure of a professional services contract. For example, a failure in the delivery of a property advisory service involving a construction project or a real estate transaction might lead to late availability of a building that is central to the service proposition.
- **Reputational damage.** This occurs as a result of such things as poor advice, loss of confidential data, conflicts of interest and so on. In the public sector, discovering that an adviser to the government on tax matters is also advising multinationals on tax avoidance schemes is embarrassing at best. Auditing is another sensitive area for both auditors and their clients.
- **Additional direct or consequential costs.** The fee structure agreed can reduce the risk of additional direct costs (see Chapter 16), but consequential costs can be substantial and because recouping them is likely to be barred under the contract, the risk of incurring them must be managed.

Classic risk management considers the probability and impact of a risk becoming a reality in order to quantify the risk. The more probable it is that an event will happen and the greater the impact on the organisation if it does, the bigger is the risk to be managed.

But as well as managing risk, skilful contract management can result in getting a greater benefit than that defined by the contract. This is most likely to be the case with a substantial project.

A framework for contract management

Table 18.1 illustrates a framework for contract management with ten separate elements, which are described below. The more the inherent risk and opportunity there is in a contract, the more effort should be put into managing it, with the different elements of the framework being given different weightings of importance according to the nature and detail of the contract.

Governance and administration

Contract governance describes the way in which contract management fits into the overall organisational control structure. Important professional services contracts should have, as well as the contract manager, a more senior executive nominated to act if required. The executive's role is to bring a more senior perspective to the contract, and act as an arbiter or help to resolve issues or problems if they arise. Efficient contract administration is crucial; original contracts and copies or backups must be stored safely, and termination and other important dates noted. A computerised database or system is not essential, but intelligent and rigorous processes and organisation are.

People

In many professional services contracts, the user, the budget holder or someone who works for them acts as the contract manager. In most instances it will be only one of their responsibilities and they may have little experience or even understanding of the role. This may not matter with a minor contract, but it will for one where risks are high and the outcome crucial. If a supplier is billing around $3m a month on a project without clear deliverables, controls or objectives, it makes sense to spend $8,000 a month on a full-time professional contract manager. One government department decided against doing so with the result that costs spiralled way above initial budgets, to the point that questions were asked by press and politicians as to what was being delivered in return for this use of taxpayers' dollars.

In larger organisations, contract management responsibility is often shared between users and the purchasing department. The user may retain operational contract management responsibility, but purchasing staff may provide guidance on governance and get involved in financial issues or in negotiating contractual changes.

Performance

A contract may define performance by describing the deliverables or key performance indicators (KPIs), in which case the contract management process must review – on a regular or continuous basis as appropriate – whether they are being delivered or met.

Where performance is being assessed throughout the life of a project, the contract should, as far as is possible and sensible, define what success looks like, and feedback to the supplier should be provided regularly in all but the briefest assignments.

A common problem with big projects is that the aims and ambitions change over time. A contract may be an easily managed fixed-price one with clear deliverables, but as the needs or aspirations of the client change it gets harder to assess performance and to manage.

There can be a reluctance to apply performance management principles to a professional services contract because of the stature of the firm or individual providing the service. But a truly professional firm, however grand it is, will be keen for there to be clarity on performance yardsticks and to have regular and constructive feedback.

Relationship (operational)

At an operational level, it is important that working relationships support effective contract management. Mechanisms that help to achieve this include regular meetings, a culture that supports honest and open discussion between the parties, rapid identification of anything that could sour the relationship, and escalation processes (referring issues to the senior manager mentioned under Governance and administration) that kick in if there are any contentious issues. In many cases, the physical proximity of client and provider helps achieve better relationships.

Payment

Payment methods can vary from a simple day rate to complex risk-reward approaches. At one extreme, payment will require little more than invoice checking and authorisation. In many cases, the purchasing organisation will need to check supplier invoices carefully. Are the hours billed reasonable and do they match any time recording evidence already provided or signed off? Are the expenses or other extras as agreed in the contract?

More complex methods, for example performance-based, risk-reward or open book (see Chapter 16), need more focus and attention. Analysis of performance may be necessary, or the auditing of a provider's information and data. Where payment mechanisms are complex, users often involve finance or purchasing colleagues in this type of activity.

Risk

Risk management plays a crucial role in engineering or construction projects. But it is nonetheless important in professional services assignments.

Some risks need to be assessed and largely managed by the buying organisation. These may be linked more to the underlying project that the professional services firm is contributing to; for instance, a big global change programme might have a risk linked to getting stakeholder acceptance across many subsidiary firms. This in turn could be a risk to the consulting firm being able to deliver its part of the project.

Some risks are best handled through joint efforts of the parties involved. The departure of key staff working for either party during the assignment is a risk that can be mitigated to some extent by both parties making sure that there is adequate staff shadowing, good documentation of activities and so on.

Contract change or development

Many projects develop or change during their lifetime. Typically, a big consulting assignment starts with some deliverables or desired outputs. But as the assignment progresses and external factors change, the deliverables or the programme of activity designed to achieve them should be reviewed and changed. Handling this well is a critical aspect of contract management.

Clear processes that define how changes can be discussed, priced (where appropriate) and agreed are essential. Where appropriate, there should be mechanisms for adjusting contractual or commercial terms in response to these changes.

At the heart of project change management are the mechanisms for assessing and quantifying the impact of changes, together with a clear governance process (who and how do changes get signed off).

Table 18.2 **Performance management framework for professional services providers**

Performance assessment of professional services providers	
Q1	Did the provider meet the objectives of the assignment?
Q2	Was the provider good to work with, open, communicative and positive in approach?
Q3	Did the provider demonstrate technical skills and knowledge?
Q4	Did the provider offer good levels of customer service (responsiveness, availability, flexibility, and so on)?
Q5	Did the provider implement skills of knowledge transfer?
Q6	Were the administrative elements of the assignment handled well by the provider (billing, reporting, and so on)?
Q7	Did the provider provide overall good value for money?
Q8	Would you use the provider again or recommend them to colleagues?
Scoring	
5	Exceeded expectations; outstanding performance
4	Met all requirements; good performance
3	Met most requirements; some minor problems; adequate performance
2	Did not meet some key requirements; disappointing performance
1	Failed to meet requirements; very poor
n/a	Not applicable to this assignment

Supplier development

Supplier development can be considered as part of "contract management" or as part of the processes described in Chapter 19; there is no clear dividing line in practical terms. For example, a supplier may have problems with invoice processing that impinge on effective contract delivery. The buyer may offer to help restructure the process to their mutual benefit. This will improve performance on this particular contract; it is also likely to help the supplier more generally and could be considered as part of a wider relationship programme.

Supplier relationship management and market management are discussed in Chapter 19.

Professional services contract management

There are particular contract management issues that apply to professional services contracts.

Difficulty in measuring

It is difficult to assess competence and capability in professional services providers, and the same applies to their performance. If a lawyer wins a case, presumably he performed well. But if he had performed even better, would the damages awarded have been greater? The change programme went well, but would a better consultant have implemented it more quickly and at lower cost? These questions are impossible to answer. But outcomes can and should be measured, particularly if the contract specifies clear deliverables. It is also possible to measure intangible factors. A structured measurement process for professional services providers such as the one shown in Table 18.2 can provide valuable information. Users or contract managers assess supplier performance after each assignment and the results are collated and fed back to providers on a quarterly or half-yearly basis. Software is now available, from both specialist providers and generalist enterprise resource planning (ERP) firms, that can help with supplier performance management and indeed wider contract management issues. Spend and provider usage (such as days worked) can be tracked, internal client feedback collected and evaluated, and useful reports produced to assist the contract or purchasing manager to keep track of suppliers' performance, costs and the overall contractual position.

Diffidence in giving feedback on performance

Many organisations and individuals – even senior people – find it hard to tell a partner in a law, consulting or audit firm that the firm's performance was unsatisfactory. So it is important to have contract managers or purchasing staff who are not afraid to do this. Guy Allen of Fujitsu (see page 73) looks for people who have strong interpersonal skills; they have to be able to hold their own with suppliers, and display determination, tenacity and independence. But above all, they have to have what he calls "intestinal fortitude". The processes described above provide a basis for an open discussion, and may make a purchasing or contract manager feel more confident when talking to that partner.

Change

This is a common feature in many professional services and other contracts. In major assignments change can be continuous, with the requirements changing from day to day. It is also a source of dissatisfaction (for both provider and purchaser) and perceived non-delivery. There are two ways of approaching change. The first is to try to head it off by not committing to a contract which incorporates change in its design.

If there is uncertainty about the later stages of a professional services assignment, commit to the work as far as there is reasonable certainty. Then re-compete when the work is done. This is how Shell handles major consulting assignments where there is uncertainty (see pages 53–5); it also ensures outputs from one phase are transferable to avoid being locked in to the provider. The second is to have a robust change process which covers early identification of issues, a transparent process for assessing the cost of change, a defined sign-off for changes, and accurate recording of changes and their implications. Much of this can be enshrined in the contract. Although it was principally designed for construction and engineering projects, the NEC3 (New Engineering Contract Edition 3), promoted by many industry and government bodies, contains elements that are applicable to professional services. Early evidence of its use on projects such as the London 2012 Olympics construction programme suggests it handles change successfully from both parties' points of view. It has a strong focus on "early warnings" and a rigorous process for handling what are termed "compensation events" that drive change.

19 Supplier relationship management

The management of suppliers of professional services stretches more broadly than plain contract management, and in the case of strategic suppliers (those that are the most critical to an organisation) is arguably more important. These days in the procurement world "supplier relationship management" (SRM) is referred to in the same way that customer relationship management (CRM) has become fashionable in the marketing world.

SRM focuses on a supplier in a context that goes beyond its operational performance on a single assignment, with the aim of securing the engagement and commitment of a supplier to gain more long-term benefit and value for the purchasing organisation.

One theme of this book is the need for purchasing staff and senior stakeholders to work together, and because professional services providers often develop relationships at a senior level in their client organisations, any successful SRM programme must have the buy-in and involvement of these stakeholders if it is to succeed. It is not something that a purchasing function can drive alone.

Although SRM programmes have become widely used over recent years, the processes are not always easy to implement, and many organisations struggle to realise the expected benefits. So it is essential to be clear about the reasons for an SRM programme and to make sure that its objectives are achievable and the outcomes are monitored. There is an argument that in a perfectly competitive market there would be no need for SRM. Purchasers would be faced with many suppliers capable of fulfilling their needs and being innovative. Thus there would be little to gain from developing strong relationships with specific suppliers. But markets are not perfect and SRM can in the right circumstances provide additional value to a purchaser that cannot be obtained purely from competent contract management.

Deciding which suppliers are strategic

The first step in an SRM programme is to segment the supply base to determine which suppliers to seek to engage with strategically. Classifying suppliers into 4–6 types or levels is usually appropriate. Each level relates to the importance and ability of the supplier to generate additional

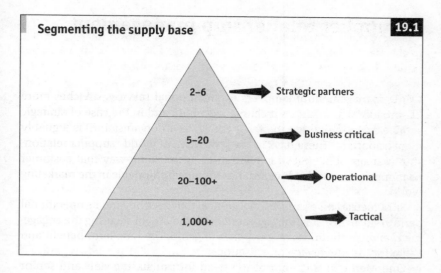

Segmenting the supply base 19.1

- 2–6 → Strategic partners
- 5–20 → Business critical
- 20–100+ → Operational
- 1,000+ → Tactical

benefits. The classification illustrated in Figure 19.1 is used by many large organisations. It divides suppliers into four levels, which in turn define how those suppliers will be managed. In most cases, only the top one or two levels will be selected for an SRM programme.

Level 1: *strategic partners*

These suppliers are essential to the strategic success of the purchasing organisation. Equally, problems with them could affect the organisation's ability to meet its objectives. Examples of possible strategic partners include:

- a professional services firm that provides strategic consulting advice and outsourced services, and is a joint-venture partner in a major overseas market;
- a subcontractor to a manufacturing firm which carries out a significant, high-value element of subassembly which includes critical intellectual property.

It is common for organisations to have 2–6 genuine strategic partners. If an organisation believes it has more than ten, it is probably overestimating their strategic importance.

Level 2: business critical suppliers

These suppliers provide goods or services that are of central importance to the work of the buying organisation, and losing or having a major problem with one of them would have serious consequences. But they are not as critical to its strategy and overall success as those in level 1. Generally, organisations have 5–20 suppliers at this level. Examples of business critical suppliers include:

- a supplier of an essential raw material for food manufacturing;
- a major IT services supplier;
- a provider of sensitive legal services, perhaps a leading global firm providing mergers and acquisitions advice across the client's organisation.

Level 3: operational suppliers

Suppliers at this level are less critical but may still provide significant quantities of goods or services. They may have some preferred supplier status, or the nature of what they provide means that there is some risk to the purchasing organisation if something went wrong. Losing such a supplier would be inconvenient but not too serious. Organisations may have anything from a handful to several hundred suppliers in this category. Examples of operational suppliers include:

- most of the providers on a consulting or legal services preferred supplier list or framework;
- a preferred office equipment supplier.

Level 4: tactical suppliers

This category includes all the other suppliers, of which there may be thousands. The assumption is that each is easy to replace and does not provide any special advantage or value. A consulting or legal firm used for a single low-value piece of work would fall into this category.

Typical professional services profile

There may be professional services providers in a firm's least critical (tactical) level, but they are likely to account for only a small amount of expenditure. At the other extreme, with big organisations at least, it is common to find professional services suppliers – such as a consulting firm that is regularly advising at board level – in the top two levels.

In selecting suppliers to be part of an SRM programme it is worth asking the question: "What will we gain from including them in a strategic supplier programme?" If that cannot be easily answered, they should not be included. And remember that providers will generally be prepared to offer additional benefits only if there is something in it for them; so value is most likely to flow where the purchasing organisation can position itself as a preferred client of the supplier. That does not mean the purchaser should be a soft touch; but it does mean that both parties must benefit from the relationship if it is to be successful.

Here is an example of effective segmentation, demonstrating the sort of providers that may be considered truly strategic in nature. For a lot of organisations there are not many providers in that category. A major international telecommunications corporation has revenues of over $5 billion. It has only two top-level "strategic partners", where it has identified opportunities for value generation though close, strategic relationships. The first is one of the world's largest IT and consulting firms. It supplies software, equipment and professional services, and also works with the international telecommunications corporation, bidding for large telecoms contracts with governments and corporations worldwide. The corporation's other strategic partner supplies equipment that is central to the business, and is one of only a handful of suppliers of that equipment in the world. Two suppliers that do not make the top-level strategic partner segment but fall into the second level of around ten business critical suppliers are the one that provides estates, property and facilities management services across the corporation and the global law firm that works on sensitive commercial issues.

Identifying the benefits

SRM programmes often fail because of the lack of clearly defined objectives against which success can be judged. Value may be extracted from a number of sources and activities which can form part of an SRM programme, and at an early stage in the process careful thought needs to be given to where that value lies.

The objective of just "improving our relationship" will not stand much scrutiny when funding is sought for an SRM programme. So it is imperative to identify achievable objectives that can be measured and lead to value creation for both parties. The examples below show the type of value that might be gained from applying SRM processes and techniques in the professional services arena. Each provider within the programme, particularly at the top strategic partner level, should be linked to a set of specific objectives.

◪ **Tacit knowledge.** Knowledge an organisation has relating to something internal or external that is not captured, codified or perhaps even recognised. It may be valuable to the purchasing organisation and the only way of gaining access to it may be through a supplier. For example, a consulting firm may have developed some ground-breaking processes that it has not yet "packaged" for the market. A preferred client may gain a competitive advantage by having early access to them.

◪ **Innovation.** This may not be freely offered by suppliers in a particular market. It may be available only through developing a close relationship with a supplier, although suppliers usually want something in return for sharing innovation. Merely being told "you are a strategic supplier" is unlikely to be enough, but explaining the benefits of what that means in practice may be.

◪ **"Free" services.** As Charles Findlay observes (see case study on page 203), when he worked as a partner in a large consulting firm, there was internal funding available to support projects that might lead to new ideas or intellectual property, and that funding could be used to provide clients involved in those projects with free or reduced-cost services. However, fee "subsidies" were offered only to clients with whom there was a strong relationship, a good level of trust and the prospect of further work. An SRM programme is designed to help develop such attributes.

◪ **Shared activities.** These might involve working together to improve processes that affect both parties, and even working together to explore joint-venture opportunities that might generate revenue for both parties. Process improvement might involve looking at how skills transfer from a professional services firm to a client can be made more effective, which would benefit the client and might lead to further business for the supplier. In terms of business development, a legal firm may have offices in countries that the purchasing organisation wishes to move into, and might consider a joint venture or sharing resources.

It is possible to combine a strong commercial approach and good outcomes in terms of price and value with strong strategic relationships. But for the relationship to be successful, the right balance has to be struck. An American carmaker was shocked to find that a Japanese-owned rival's new model contained an innovative gearbox, provided by one of the American firm's suppliers. When the American firm asked why it had not been offered this product, the supplier explained that the relationship with the Japanese firm was based on long-term mutual success, and the customer was happy for the supplier to make a decent profit. Although the American firm was supposedly committed to effective supplier relationship management, for many years its purchasing focus had been on taking cost out, often at the expense of its suppliers or cash available for development. That the Japanese carmaker had played some role in the development of the product had strengthened the strategic relationship between the two firms.

It is also true that benefits can be obtained without huge cost through developing strong relationships. Merely praising a supplier can be highly motivating and encourage performance improvement.

Running a successful programme

Once the objectives of an SRM programme are clear, four aspects of the programme should be considered:

- **Resources.** Many SRM programmes that were seen as an add-on to operational contract management have failed through being under-resourced. Evidence also suggests that managers responsible for SRM programmes need to be adept in the softer management skills such as influencing and relationship building, as well as possessing tenacity and being focused on results. That mix of skills is not perhaps found in a typical purchasing or contract manager. One global oil firm has recruited heavily from the sales and marketing world for members of its successful SRM team.
- **Programme management.** The chances of an SRM programme working well are higher if it is managed tightly according to a formal structure, with actions, deliverables and resource levels clearly defined. A senior manager needs to take formal ownership of the programme and to drive the commitment and energy needed if it is to be successful, and an operational level programme manager should have responsibility for making things happen.
- **Stakeholder engagement and governance.** SRM rarely succeeds in the absence of stakeholder involvement, and in professional services, strategic suppliers, who are senior external stakeholders, will have senior internal stakeholders. Often, a board director is appointed for each supplier in an SRM programme to interact at that level with a counterpart from the supplier. But this must not become a board members' social club. Expensive quarterly lunches

may be fine, but only if part of a structured SRM programme. The test of success is to look at documented agendas, discussion notes and outcomes from such meetings. If get-togethers, whether over lunch or elsewhere, are not structured in that way, they are likely to have limited value.

◾ **Deliverables and measures.** The ends that justify the programme and the resources committed to it. Not only do the objectives of an SRM programme have to be defined, but so too do the measures to be used to determine whether they have been achieved.

Beyond SRM: market management

SRM focuses on a particular supplier or group of suppliers, and moves beyond the individual contract or contracts. In the context of the end-to-end purchasing cycle, it is almost the last step. The next, and final, step in taking a strategic purchasing view is post-contract market consideration and management.

Purchasing staff will generally consider the market at the early stages of a category management process (see Chapter 9). What is sometimes forgotten is the need to continue that market analysis, and a level of awareness and review, once contracts are up and running. Understanding activities or changes in the market, the capability of suppliers, including new market entrants, or technological developments is important in the context of the buying organisation's needs.

Market awareness can be gained in a number of ways, including:

◾ industry research, news and information;
◾ latest developments from suppliers, directly or through sources such as websites;
◾ market events, conferences and exhibitions;
◾ Dun & Bradstreet or similar services (for example, continuous reporting of suppliers' financial announcements and monitoring of their financial strength and business position).

This closes the loop of the end-to-end process. Research and awareness through the contract delivery period feed into the next round of contracting, whether as part of a three-year cycle of awarding framework contracts to a range of suppliers, or more directly as a series of one-off contracts. Considering the market and supply options should be a continuous process, not a sudden shock every three years when contracts are about to expire.

Ten tips for supplier relationship management

1 **Get the priorities right.** Once a contract is in place it is essential to know how suppliers perform against it. Only when the basics are in place should you think about more sophisticated SRM processes.
2 **Choose the suppliers carefully.** Few organisations have the resources to do effective SRM with hundreds or even dozens of suppliers. It is better to succeed with a handful of suppliers, then grow, than to bite off more than you can chew.
3 **Relate SRM to the organisation's objectives.** Work with suppliers to achieve better value for money, or innovation, or to develop approaches to new markets. The programme must link to the organisation's goals.
4 **Consider the supplier.** Understand what suppliers want out of the relationship and set your objectives accordingly. An SRM programme will succeed only with supplier co-operation; there must therefore be real benefit.
5 **Put in the effort.** Don't underestimate the resources needed for SRM. Be prepared for this or don't bother.
6 **Data is important.** Don't get obsessed by it but you will need a clear view of your business with the supplier, spending patterns, and so on.
7 **Involve internal stakeholders.** SRM can't be a purely technical or procurement based activity. The "people" side of things is important and you need everyone working to the agreed agenda.
8 **Allocate responsibility carefully.** Consider who is best placed to handle different aspects of SRM. This may not be the purchasing or contract manager.
9 **Be creative in your approach.** Involve suppliers in product development. Many different techniques, tools and processes can be used.
10 **Have a fall-back.** However close you are now, this supplier might not meet your needs in the future, or may even decide to become a competitor. Remember that relationships don't last forever, and in parallel to SRM, you need to be thinking about the contingency of other strategies and suppliers.

Charles Findlay explains below how clients can get more out of their suppliers, and how as a result of developing strong relationships clients may be able to obtain a level of value from suppliers that is above and beyond the letter of the contract.

Accenture

Like many of the people interviewed for this book, Charles Findlay has sat on both sides of the fence. He worked for Accenture for 15 years, ending up as a partner in its European supply chain consulting practice. He also ran Accenture's procurement outsourcing business and had responsibility for purchasing at one stage. He left in 2005, and is now a business angel, investing in and working with small firms, and a top-level consultant for various organisations.

Over the years, Findlay has learned much about how organisations can get the most out of their suppliers, particularly professional services firms. The first thing he does is draw a distinction between assignments that have clear deliverables, particularly fixed-price assignments, and those that are more time and materials based. He explains:

If the assignment is suitable for a fixed price, the value comes in getting the specification accurate and clear and having a strong procurement and contracting process. That will capture most of the value. Contract and supplier management can then focus on ensuring the supplier delivers what it has promised; it still requires some skill, but it is relatively straightforward. But for an assignment that is basically time and material based, the two main factors are the relationship between client and provider, and management of the provider's resource.

Relationships are crucial, Findlay has found, based on his experience on both the buyer and supplier side of the fence. As a partner at Accenture, he led a major procurement change assignment for a large organisation. His client, the purchasing director, insisted on having lunch with him at least once a fortnight, but it was not just to exchange pleasantries:

He spent every lunch pumping me for information, my views not just on the assignment we were delivering, but other issues he was facing. He got tens of thousands of pounds of free advice from me over these non-billable lunches. Other clients see the meeting with the partner as a formality and it is just a quick coffee. It can be much more.

His experience highlights what can be gained from the relationship aspect of supplier management. Findlay continues:

This client also persuaded us to do "development" work at low or no cost. There was always the prospect of more work: clearly, few consulting firms would be prepared to provide this sort of added value if that wasn't the case. But many clients just don't develop the relationships or push to see what additional value they could get from their provider once that relationship is established.

In terms of motivating the provider, he sees the prospect of future business as the main driver for most professional services firms:

There is every chance of getting your provider to sign up to almost anything reasonable on a risk-reward basis if they see the prospect of more work ahead.

But he also cautions that measuring outcomes and benefits can be difficult and has led to some tricky contractual discussions about risk-reward outcomes:

And risk-reward needs to be pitched in the right way so it doesn't lead to dysfunctional behaviour.

Findlay sees resource management as another aspect of successful supplier management:

This same client always said we could bring anyone we wanted onto the assignment: he trusted me to judge who had the right skills. But we still had a monthly review with him when we went through every one of our consultants individually. Anyone who wasn't pulling their weight would be removed from the assignment, so that kept our minds focused on delivering real and continuous value.

Findlay sees this particular purchasing director as an excellent role model for others.

He also understood our business model as well as I did, and knew when we were busy or quiet. He used that in his negotiations with us. I've come across some charlatans in the consulting industry who will steal intellectual property rather than develop their own, and who aren't really interested in the client. But most firms want to do the right thing, and it really does help to have a client who makes the effort to understand the market and how providers operate, and who is prepared to build a mutually successful relationship.

20 Sustainability and corporate social responsibility

O ver recent years, the range of factors that have been taken into account in purchasing has broadened considerably. Buyers have long been aware of the need to balance price with wider criteria such as the quality of what they were buying, or the service offered by the supplier. From this an awareness of whole-life costs has gradually developed. A car might be cheap to buy, but fuel consumption, too-frequent breakdowns and poor residual value when it is sold in five years' time may make it expensive on a whole-life basis. Today, however, even more complex issues – those to do with corporate social responsibility or CSR – are involved in purchasing decisions.

Sustainability is even harder to define in a business context than CSR, yet it too has become an important factor for purchasing and other business people to consider. The Earth Charter speaks of "a sustainable global society founded on respect for nature, universal human rights, economic justice, and a culture of peace". More practically, sustainability in a context such as purchasing means looking beyond merely immediate value for money for the purchaser and taking into account the issues that affect wider society, now and in the future.

The Institute of Supply Management, based in the United States, in *Principles of Sustainability and Social Responsibility*, comments:

> *Supply base diversity and inclusiveness arise from efforts to engage different categories of suppliers in sourcing processes and decisions. In this context:*
> - *Provide socially diverse suppliers the opportunity to participate in sourcing opportunities.*
> - *Promote inclusion of diverse suppliers in the organisation's supplier development and mentoring programs.*
> - *Ensure long-term program sustainability through application of forward thinking concepts beyond price.*

This is a good summary of the principal issues. Another approach is to consider three main elements as forming the basis for CSR:

◪ **Environmental sustainability.** Ensuring that the goods and services they buy meet environmental standards and contribute towards a sustainable approach has become part of the purchasing role in large organisations in both the private and state sectors. This involves:
- using materials that do not have negative environmental impacts, such as ensuring wood used to make paper or furniture comes from sustainable sources such as managed forests;
- implementing measures to reduce an organisation's carbon footprint;
- taking into account whole-life costs when purchasing, including running and disposal costs; for example, electrical equipment, where full-life running costs can be many times the initial purchase price.

◪ **Social sustainability.** Organisations have legal obligations in many countries (such as the Civil Rights Act in the United States and the Race Relations Act in the UK) not to discriminate on the basis of race, sex, creed, colour, age or disability. Purchasing from offshore sources has come under the spotlight. The use of sweatshops or child labour to produce goods sold in the developed world has been highly damaging for the western firms whose suppliers have been involved. In professional services, offshoring is playing an increasing role, and although back-office operations in developing countries may operate to high standards, buyers should be aware of how outsourced services are being provided and take appropriate steps to ensure that their suppliers are acting properly at all times.

◪ **Economic sustainability.** This is probably the least understood of these topics. It has been expressed in some quarters for instance as a preference for buying locally, which is contentious as it can be seen as perilously close to economic protectionism. But there are genuine opportunities; for instance, buyers can encourage genuinely innovative new and small businesses, whose growth and success may have wider benefits to the economy and the community.

Professional services and CSR

Big retailers and others have taken on board that their customers now expect them to behave responsibly and to take steps to make sure their suppliers do too. The reputational risk of not doing so is potentially huge.

Professional services firms, however, have some way to go on some CSR issues. For example, the proportion of ethnic minority staff at senior levels in many law firms in western Europe is still far below their representation in the community generally. In the UK, a 2006 survey of the leading 100 law firms revealed that there were no ethnic minority partners in one-third of the firms involved. In the United States, a 2009 study of 46 Washington law firms with more than 100 attorneys revealed that in 28 firms fewer than 3% of the partners were black and seven firms had no black partners. Nationally, about 5% of law firm partners are black, compared with 13.5% black Americans in the general population.

The purchasing department's role

Organisations should be aware of these issues and the positive steps that can be taken to address them. As the UK's Office of Government Commerce, which lays down guidelines on public procurement, puts it:

> *Reaching out to the widest possible range of contractors – including, for example, those owned by people from ethnic minority communities, women and disabled people – ensures access to suppliers who can offer real benefits and help deliver these personalised goods and services. There is also an opportunity to work with suppliers to influence their equality practices and achieve greater transparency. Encouraging the creation of workplaces with open and effective equality practices helps contractors drive up productivity, through attracting recruits from the widest pool, better staff retention, and improved morale and performance. Suppliers can consequently ensure the best people are delivering the services procured. Considering equalities issues in procurement is therefore not only about satisfying legal obligations ... It can also help public procurers deliver higher-quality services and achieve better value for money in procurement activities.*

In the widest sense, CSR should be kept in mind at each stage of the purchasing process. Below are steps that can be taken to promote CSR.

Pre-procurement

Diversity in the supplier base can be encouraged by appropriate packaging of contracts. Frameworks (see Chapter 10) can be constructed to bring smaller or niche firms into the picture, or there could be a flexible approach to lower value contracts that allows the use of non-framework smaller or niche firms.

Specification

CSR requirements can be included in the specification for the assignment. For example, in the case of a consulting study for a state-owned organisation, this involved interviewing individuals from minority ethnic groups. The purchasing director running the project explains:

> We felt it appropriate to specify that staff involved from the professional services firm should receive diversity training before they engaged with the public.

Selection

Selection criteria can be linked to CSR; for example, firms could be asked about the specific actions they are taking on CSR. But it should be noted that under EU purchasing regulations, all evaluation criteria used for selecting suppliers must be relevant to the contract. As the UK Office of Government Commerce points out:

> Equality issues can be considered when looking at a potential supplier's technical ability to perform a contract where they are relevant to that particular contract. For example, a contract may require specific know-how or skills relating to equality issues, such as language skills or cultural awareness for services that are to be delivered to diverse communities, in which case public authorities can ask for evidence of the skills or know-how.

A purchasing manager at an American finance firm explained her approach:

> We awarded a recent contract for management consulting where we asked a selection question about the recruitment and training of staff, a quite normal area to investigate to help establish the capability of the bidding firms. But we added to the standard question by asking how the firms selected their consultants to achieve the right skills and capability while ensuring that the selection was independent of colour, race or creed. That seemed to us a reasonable question and one that might challenge a few firms to think about their recruitment policies.

The contract

Contracts can be constructed to point suppliers in the right direction on CSR. But once again the terms and conditions must be relevant to the performance of the contract; if not, the buyer may incur additional costs without much tangible benefit. For example, a legal services firm may be carrying out administrative functions in other countries and a purchaser may wish to stipulate conditions in the contract, such as conditions for workers in such countries or the right to inspect premises. In other cases, the contractual conditions may simply highlight legislative requirements and provide sanctions for the buyer if the provider does not adhere to these conditions.

Contract management

Adherence to contractual conditions that are relevant to CSR issues – such as a requirement that consultants receive diversity training – should be monitored in the same way as other contract terms.

Relationship management

Other issues that may be addressed through the supplier management process could include encouraging suppliers to look at their own supplier base in the light of CSR issues. For instance, one major UK government department has successfully encouraged a number of suppliers, including some in the professional services sector, to consider both employing more disabled staff and buying goods manufactured by "supported businesses" which employ disabled staff. If there is a strategic supplier relationship programme (see Chapter 19), this can be used to encourage CSR. For instance, can the purchaser and supplier work together to reduce their environmental impact? What is the flow of paper between the supplier and the purchasing organisation? Can this be reduced with environmental benefit? How many face-to-face meetings take place? Can some be changed to videoconferencing to reduce travel? It may not be appropriate to make such issues contractual, but action in these areas can be encouraged through non-contractual targets or as part of supplier management activities.

PART 7
CONCLUSIONS

Many of the problems that arise in professional services projects originate in the purchasing process. Expectations may be unrealistic and the scope of the project may not be defined sufficiently clearly. Suppliers may be selected on the basis of personal relationships and past experience, even when neither is relevant to the project in hand. However, problems also arise during the project itself: the buying organisation may not make the contribution to the project it has promised; the professional services firm may focus too much on trying to sell the next piece of work.

Successful professional services work depends both on commitment and clear communication from the senior people who have commissioned the project, and on effective working relationships between the client's staff and the advisers at junior, as well as senior, levels.

These factors, together with a more intelligent approach to buying, will become more important in the future, as the professional services industry is threatened by greater regulation, falling margins and structural change.

21 What makes a successful assignment?

Professional service assignments break down into two broad categories: those you have to buy and those you choose to buy. Non-discretionary and discretionary projects share "top-down" factors that are critical to success, but discretionary projects require something more, an approach that incorporates "bottom-up" factors as well.

Top-down success factors

When an organisation hires a professional services firm because it has to (for a statutory audit, to provide legal advice in an important case, or to replace an outdated IT system), it will have a specific outcome in mind. Success therefore does not relate to a vague idea of exceeding expectations – the benchmark many services are measured against – but to the achievement of this objective.

Doing that depends largely on expert knowledge: the auditor needs to be qualified; the lawyer needs to have knowledge of relevant case law and precedent; the IT consultant needs to have experience of new systems. In a 2007 survey carried out by the UK's Management Consultancies Association (MCA), 74% of the people questioned who were satisfied with the work done by consultants thought the consultants knew what they were talking about, compared with just 17% of dissatisfied respondents (the remaining 9% were neither satisfied nor dissatisfied). But it is not just the knowledge of the adviser that matters. In the survey, the people who were satisfied were far more likely to have invested in the preparatory stages of a project, gathering information themselves so that the consultants could hit the ground running.

Non-discretionary projects are inherently easier to manage and are therefore more likely to achieve their stated aims, largely because of the high level of technical expertise required:

- Those involved on the client side are more likely to be experts. This makes the buying process easier (the client is better placed to evaluate the professional services firm's expertise) and the working relationships more comfortable (experts respect each other).
- Because the client is clear about what is needed – technical

expertise to achieve a specific objective – there is less internal debate about bringing the advisers in.

◻ The smaller number of people involved on the client side means that many of the problems that bedevil larger-scale projects with integrated client-adviser teams do not apply.

Discretionary projects have to grapple with additional complexities:

◻ The nature of the expertise to be provided by the professional services firm may be less clearly defined, making it harder for people to recognise and value the expertise they encounter.

◻ The level of expertise on the client side is often unclear. If someone is not sure what skills and experience are required, it may be thought, rightly or wrongly, that they exist within the organisation and so there is ambivalence and a lack of consensus on bringing in outsiders.

◻ Equally, if clients are unsure what skills are needed, they can do little to prepare or train themselves for using the advisers. This can lead to clients relying on advisers to tell them whether other advisers are up to the job.

In such circumstances, when bringing external advisers into an organisation there must be:

◻ **A clear sense of purpose.** Clarity is something those who bring in professional advisers preach, but do not always practice. Not surprisingly, decision-makers, because they are typically the people who bring advisers in, are clear about the objectives. Those lower down the organisational hierarchy may be less so.

◻ **Commitment from the top.** For a project to succeed, it has to be clear to all those involved that senior management is behind the project and fully backs it.

◻ **Communication.** Both the clear sense of purpose and top-level commitment have to be visible to the rest of the organisation. Senior executives cannot leave it up to middle and junior managers to decide what to say about the involvement of external advisers in a project.

Bottom-up factors

Commitment, a clear sense of purpose and communication are all hugely

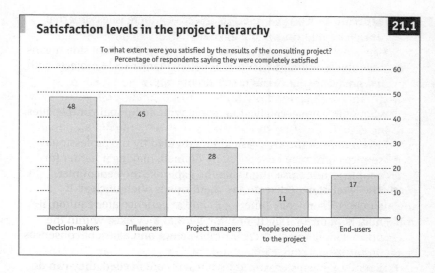

Satisfaction levels in the project hierarchy `21.1`

To what extent were you satisfied by the results of the consulting project?
Percentage of respondents saying they were completely satisfied

important but they are top-down factors. It is the senior people who have to be credible, committed, know what they are doing and be able to communicate it. Junior people are merely told what is going on and what to do.

Perhaps because there is so much emphasis on the top-down approach, the more senior people are, the more likely they are to be satisfied. Decision-makers often view consulting projects positively (see Figure 21.1) because this validates their decision to use consultants; it may also be that they are in a better position to see the overall benefits. People seconded to projects from elsewhere in an organisation may resent the consultants' presence because they were not involved in the original decision to bring them in and do not understand the rationale for doing so.

This research was based on consulting projects, but the same would be true for any discretionary work, whether it is an audit firm reviewing a crucial project or a tax consultancy benchmarking a multinational's approach to transfer pricing. The professional services industry should be concerned about this because it is the level of engagement among people who work with advisers that determines success in most discretionary projects.

There are three facets to this kind of collaborative success:

◪ Integrated teams. Professional projects that go well usually involve a joint client–consultant team.

- Flexibility. In discretionary projects it is often not just people's experience that counts, but also their ability to think on their feet.
- Individuals and organisations should benefit. Joint working and not imposing a rigid methodology are important to people working with consultants, but the crucial factor is the extent to which the people involved on the client side gain something from the experience. Why should they put up with the disruption of having consultants in if they do not benefit?

That no one gets out of bed on a Monday morning to improve their employer's share price is a truism of modern management, so why should anyone expect the people involved in discretionary projects to think any differently? What is in it for them?

David Shields of the UK Office of Government Commerce explains below what he believes clients (and the UK government in particular) need to do to manage professional services providers better. He also looks to the future and a time of government spending constraints, and explains how he thinks providers need to develop if they are to meet the changing needs of clients.

UK Office of Government Commerce

Lean, casually dressed and brimming with energy, David Shields is an example of a new breed of public-sector manager. Before joining the Office of Government Commerce (OGC), which oversees all expenditure by central government in the UK, he had had extensive experience in the private sector, in both general management and procurement. He now runs the OGC's collaborative procurement programme where he is responsible for delivering savings in expenditure categories that are common in UK public-sector purchasing. He explains:

> We look at nine categories including areas such as car fleets, energy, IT and office solutions, as well as professional services. Total spending across our target categories is around £80 billion a year.

However, the OGC has no direct authority over the government departments and agencies, local authorities, hospitals, educational establishments and police forces it works with. So influencing and persuading the principal stakeholders, both procurement people and budget holders, is a fundamental part of the role:

Of course there is room for local purchasing in many areas, but in some categories there are clear benefits from understanding demand and leveraging cross-government expenditure.

It is hard to make progress without knowing who is spending what and with whom, and it has taken time to extract the data needed to approach the market in an informed way:

But we're getting there, particularly in terms of data from central government organisations, and we are seeing real results and benefits in many areas.

The Consultancy Value Programme (CVP), set up by the OGC with the Home Office as the pilot customer, has played a central role in getting to grips with the professional services category. Shields explains:

The CVP has a number of strands. Demand management is vital; ensuring organisations have appropriate controls on the use of consultants. Getting people to look at what resources are available internally is the first option. Understanding the market and different types of providers, their strengths and weaknesses, is also critical: we want people to think about what they need, not how the professional services providers define their offerings. We also found that many buyers did not understand how consulting firms are organised, or their business models, something we think is essential if they're to use the levers for gaining better value as a customer.

So the drive has not been to try to negotiate cross-government "mega-deals" but to educate procurement staff and disseminate information about provider performance and capability. Shields says:

That seems key to me. For instance, we need to distinguish between the capability held at firm level and that held by individuals. Which is most important for the buyer? We need to assess how both people and firms perform and to ensure that colleagues around the public sector share that knowledge, for instance by reusing the intellectual property we've already paid for. And if we find a tremendous adviser working in one public organisation, let's try and make sure we get him or her on the project when that firm is engaged elsewhere.

It is also necessary to weed out poor performers. Shields's personal experience of managing professional services providers comes into play here:

If you are honest and prepared to be direct, you can quickly make sure you have a truly high-performing individual or team working on your account. You shouldn't tolerate mediocrity. It may be someone doesn't have the cultural fit; it may not always be a question of pure ability; but if I'm paying adviser rates, I want consistently excellent performance.

What about the use of frameworks, now prevalent in the public sector? Shields's view is that they have a place in terms of convenience, time savings and value:

But of course procurement people shouldn't use them unthinkingly. Local procurement people need to take an active role within their organisations in understanding the business drivers and the needs of their users; they need to be involved in issues early so they can make strategic sourcing decisions about supply options. That should include whether they use a framework or go to market. Using a framework should not be a reflex reaction.

Shields has no doubt that better expenditure data and the CVP are having an impact:

Our figures show a 40% decrease in consultancy expenditure among central government departments in 2007/08. We're also seeing a better understanding of the market and more informed negotiations. But of course we can do better.

What about the future? There is already considerable political sensitivity concerning the use of consultants in the public sector and this is likely to increase as overall public spending is cut back. Shields is realistic:

I can see consultancy spend declining, but many government programmes need specialist external expertise or an injection of high-level resource. Our role is to make sure that money is spent to the best possible effect to implement the government's policy goals.

What about the supply side? Shields has considered this carefully:

A few years ago, the large IT firms had fairly diverse offerings; hardware, services, solutions weren't particularly joined up. Now the biggest and best have become much better at offering clients integrated services and solutions. The major consulting firms are where IT providers were ten years ago: too many still offer us a range of services that may be good in each of their silos but aren't integrated. I may want some strategic consulting, tied into some operational delivery on more of an outsourced basis, with occasional interim-type support. And I may want to speak to a single supplier about that. Most consulting firms have strong individual offerings; but there is little joined-up thinking and it's hard to engage them in that debate. That is even more important as "consulting" firms blur the boundaries and move into outsourcing and other delivery areas.

Shields sums up:

It is frustrating at times having limited direct control, but we feel we are doing something worthwhile, the scale, impact and potential benefits both financial and in terms of delivering frontline services are huge, and it's hard to think of a bigger challenge in procurement.

22 What could possibly go wrong?

Earlier chapters focused on good practice and getting the best possible results and value from professional services expenditure, with a focus on what can be done to achieve success. Using the experiences of senior executives, this chapter describes some of the major problems and common causes of assignment failure; in effect the consequences of not getting things right.

Initial design of the assignment

Many of the problems that occur have their origins in the very early stages of the purchasing process; when the initial design and specification of the assignment are being determined.

Unrealistic expectations

These are common and can easily lead to clients feeling that they have not obtained what they wanted from the assignment. They can also leave suppliers with a vague sense of resentment; they feel aggrieved that they have delivered what they thought was wanted, yet the client is clearly not happy.

A category manager described receiving a report that did not go into the detail wanted or cover many of the issues:

> It didn't live up to the impressive proposal and fancy presentation we got from the consultants when they pitched for the work.

This can be the client's or the advisers' fault, or a bit of both. It is easy to have unrealistic expectations of a consultant. Buyers ask for a proposal, and when the consultant works out a detailed plan that costs $100,000, the buyer or budget holder says, "that's too expensive". Then the consultant de-scopes the project, in effect developing a plan to do less work. But the buyer often still expects the full output and is let down by the finished product.

Sometimes the consultant plays up to these unrealistic expectations and suggests that everything can be achieved for just $50,000. Clients assume that because consultants smile nicely and say they understand their needs, this is enough to lead to a great final product. It is not. Detailed, written agreement about what is to be delivered is crucial in most cases. A successful assignment needs both parties to play their part, with clarity on what is going to be delivered. The purchasing organisation must be clear about what is required and specify the output; and the supplier must make it clear if it cannot deliver what is wanted for the price offered. If a report covering topics A, B and C, 20–30 pages long, is what is wanted, tell the supplier that. But do not expect the earth if your budget is only $10,000.

Lack of deliverables

Perhaps the most common type of problem with professional services assignments is engaging advisers without clear deliverables, outputs or goals. "We need some consultants" is the cry from the client organisation and some are engaged – but before there is a clear definition of what is wanted from them.

This is most common where a single assignment is badly defined, or not defined at all. There are also examples of similar problems where advisers have been engaged on a retainer basis, perhaps to provide "as and when" advice on a particular issue through the year for a fixed fee. A senior marketing director described a firm of public relations consultants, paid a six-figure annual retainer, who when challenged after some years to define what they had delivered over the previous year listed three press releases as their total contribution.

But the fault lay with the client as much as the consultant. A retainer arrangement can work well, but a clear set of activities, deliverables or outputs should still be expected as part of that; or indeed some mechanism for adjusting cost if the work does not materialise.

Unexpected magnitude of costs

A purchasing manager in the food industry told of his shock the first time he used the firm that provided his corporation with legal advice on complex contracts:

> I naively assumed that I would get some limited advice free of charge as I understood we had a corporate arrangement. And the lawyer was very helpful, and gave good advice.

A month later, when he received an invoice for $2,000 for what he perceived had been a couple of quick phone calls and two e-mails, he learnt the truth. He admits:

It was my fault. I was inexperienced, but particularly as a
purchasing man, I really should have asked the right questions.

Without a contract, purchase order or even a letter of agreement, he was on shaky ground to argue with the lawyer. And, to be fair, she may have been acting in good faith; she may have carried out considerable research to support his enquiry, for instance. If he did not specify exactly what was wanted and the cost of it, or even give an indication of the expected costs, she may not have realised the cost expectation was much lower. Or she may just have exploited his lack of commercial awareness.

Even if you cannot specify the work exactly, it is a good idea to let the lawyers know your expectations of cost; or tell them that they must inform you when they their costs hit, say, $1,000. Even better, agree a fixed price for the work.

Supplier selection and negotiation
The following issues arise during or because of the supplier selection and contract negotiation phases of the purchasing process.

The wrong choice
Providers should be selected in a structured and thoughtful manner. Common mistakes include selecting a provider based on their processes or methodologies without focusing enough on the people who will be providing the advice; or selecting on the basis of previous work done for the client rather than fully examining competence in the specific area required for the assignment. One CFO comments:

We found our usual lawyers, who were excellent at contractual
and human resources advice, just weren't in the same league
when it came to advising on mergers and acquisitions.

Internal disconnect
It is important to get purchasing people and users of professional services working together successfully. Where that does not happen, the result can be poor outcomes.

A purchasing director at a large multinational company put in place a framework of consulting firms, then found a year later that well over half the spend on consulting was still going to other suppliers:

In retrospect, we didn't spend long enough finding out what sort of firms our users really wanted. So many of them just ignore our framework and continue to do their own thing.

That director was honest enough to admit his own failings. But on other occasions, colleagues just may not want to accept purchasing discipline. If that is the case, the issue should be raised at a higher level, and real governance on the engagement of professional services firms may be needed to control this "maverick" behaviour.

In some cases, the purchasing department may have considerable power or influence but may not use it in an appropriate manner. A badly designed selection process, without the right level of user input, may result in the selection of a firm that cannot meet the user's needs.

Ineffective negotiation: in either direction

Weak negotiation can end up with the client paying more than is necessary or the market requires. But equally, simply beating the supplier over the head can have dysfunctional outcomes. As Jason Busch of Spend Matters and Azul Partners puts it:

> *In my experience, if you beat up firms too hard on day rate, they will get you back in other ways. You will just find less good people are put onto the project, or it takes twice as long. What the best clients in the United States are doing is aligning their advisers with the value they get from the work, through risk-reward or similar mechanisms.*

In professional services, in most cases negotiation needs to be on a collaborative basis (see Chapter 14). A balance needs to be struck between driving a good deal and achieving an outcome that makes the provider want to do the work to the best of its ability.

Project delivery and contract management

Martin Webb, who has worked as a chief purchasing officer (CPO) for many years in the telecommunications sector, highlights how it is clients who are sometimes responsible for problems or failings:

> *It is essential that consulting assignments have senior-level support, unless the consultants are just being set up to fail and take the blame. But surprisingly, many organisations still don't see consultants as real assets to be fully utilised.*

The dithering client

One senior consultant described a particular financial services assignment:

> They just didn't know what they wanted. I thought I understood,
> but every time we had a meeting, it seemed they wanted us to do
> something else. And it wasn't just the content of the work; even
> the style of engagement was uncertain. One day they wanted
> my team to be tough and independent, the next they were
> annoyed if we expressed doubts about their project.

This can happen because clients do not have a clear view of what they want out of an assignment, or because the desired outcomes or deliverables change rapidly or regularly in an uncontrolled manner. Sometimes consultants are just outlets for clients' frustration – when they have had a bad day they can kick the adviser, but they cannot kick their staff or the boss. That does not make it right, and it is a poor use of clients' money. Advisers have a choice: do they smile and take the cash, or insist on clear deliverables and a documented change process with senior governance?

The disappearing client

Worse than clients who are unable to make up their minds at meetings are those who do not show up for meetings in the first place. A 2009 survey by sourceforconsulting.com of more than 30 consulting projects found that 40% of project overruns were caused by problems that arose during the project. Two of the most important were the failure of clients to provide information or other resources that had been promised to the consulting firm, and difficulties in getting time in the diaries of senior people on the client side. One consultant who responded to the survey said that, in a three-month project, the client had been too busy to have a meeting before the end of the second month. Another recalled working on a "joint" client-consultant team in which nine of the ten people on the client side were independent contractors, not full-time employees.

It does not make sense to have an expensive consultant or lawyer sitting around wasting time because a meeting cannot be arranged or someone has failed to arrive, particularly when advisers may well be "on the clock", charging the client for their time.

Scope creep and the everlasting project

The CPO of a government agency told of a number of "one man band" consultants who had worked for her organisation virtually full-time for over five years. In some cases, they were originally engaged for short assignments of a few weeks' duration. "But there was always something more for them to do." The same can happen in larger firms; various clients over the years have been accused of being unable to make any strategic decisions without McKinsey, Bain or whoever at their side. This sort of client becomes a valuable annuity for the consulting firm.

There is often a temptation for firms to extend and draw out assignments. Clients get used to having the consultants around. They are a useful resource, and they are bright people who do not go sick or cause problems in the office as often as salaried staff. So relationships continue sometimes long after it is sensible for either party. The solution is for the client to define what is wanted up front and be prepared to say "thanks and goodbye" when it is achieved. If drift is occurring, take stock of the assignment, set clear deliverables for what is still outstanding, agree a plan, cost and timing with the consultant for getting them delivered, make sure the agreed activities happen, then shake hands and part amicably.

Upwards selling

A manager at a footwear company says:

> The most annoying thing I've ever experienced is the consultant who was clearly not interested in me or my $100,000 assignment, but spent all his time trying to get appointments with my boss or even his boss. He wanted the million-dollar assignment and that got in the way of what he was supposed to be delivering for me.

This is a common complaint about the behaviour of professional advisers, sometimes called "sell-on". Professional services firms' business models are usually based on staff utilisation; so particularly when times are tough, senior consultants and partners are under great pressure to get more of their colleagues working on existing accounts. A client needs to respond firmly. If you are the budget holder and have authority, tell the consultants that if this continues you will fire them. Insist that they contact your boss (or his boss) only with your knowledge and permission. If you do not have that power, at least make your feelings clear. The consultants may be getting in to see your boss, but presumably they would not be happy if you told your boss what a poor job they were doing. Keep that threat up your sleeve.

Personal positioning

The head of procurement for a UK government department says:

> I didn't believe it was happening at first. A consulting firm was
> helping us design our new organisation structure. I discovered
> that one of their consultants was actually positioning himself for
> the job in the new structure that I thought was earmarked for me.

This is more common than you might think. In this case the internal
director left, but the consultant did not get the job. If this is happening, it is
reasonable to fire the consulting firm, or at least the consultant concerned.
If you do not have the power to do that, the outcome will depend on the
strength of your relationship with your boss. Indeed, your boss may want
you out; that possibility should be considered. But at least speak to the
consultant's partner confidentially and express your unhappiness.

23 The future of professional services

The focus of this book has been how to buy professional services in the context of the current market. But the sector is changing, in some areas rapidly. Current concerns about the return on investment for such services may force professional services firms to look for ways to quantify their impact and value. Public criticism, especially if exacerbated by major scandals, may open the door to increased regulation. Falling fee rates and margins may force firms to carry out more of their work in low-cost locations overseas. Clients may choose to involve several firms in a single project, forcing firms to work together. Such changes may have a substantial impact, not just on professional services firms themselves, but also on the way organisations buy and use their services in the future.

Scenario 1: the measure of value

One of the principal themes of this book has been that because of intangible factors it can be difficult to determine the value professional services should and do in practice deliver. With the more standardised services, people are clearer about what they are buying, but where a service is tailored to fit a client's circumstances, it is hard to identify and measure the contribution made by professional advisers. The need to define value increases according to the amount of choice there is. If a client has to buy a particular service, such as a statutory audit, valuing it has little merit; the focus will be on the quality of the work and the efficiency of its delivery. However, being able to compare the value of the other services offered by accounting firms, such as tax or internal audit consulting, is much more important and would be a factor in selecting one. Similarly, most consulting work is discretionary: because clients do not have to commission consulting projects, they are often more concerned about the value they will receive.

The difficulty of defining value poses as many problems to suppliers as it does to buyers. If buyers cannot defend their purchase decision based on a clear return on investment, suppliers will struggle to stimulate demand because they cannot prove their worth. Consulting firms are leading the field in terms of response; Bain, for example, compares the performance of its clients against that of the market as a whole. Research by the Management Consultancies Association in 2010 looked at value from three perspectives: the direct impact consulting firms have on the economy, in terms of not just tax paid, but also training, research and pro bono work for charities; levels of client satisfaction; and the value added during the course of a project, calculated as the multiple of the fees paid. But even in this most discretionary of professional services, there is no agreement as yet on a sensible, even standard, approach.

Professional services firms and industry bodies are therefore likely to put more effort in future into determining the value they add through, for example, more systematic and regular satisfaction surveys, the use of tools such as the balanced scorecard to define how value will be added at the start of a project, and a greater willingness to offer performance-related fees.

These efforts, however, will not solve the underlying problem, partly because they will be too project-specific to allow clients to compare the value created by one firm with that of another. Buyers, on their part, may decide to exchange more information about the performance of suppliers and may even be willing to contribute to league tables or surveys that compare firms on a variety of different dimensions, much like the Thomson Reuters Extel Survey, which aims to benchmark excellence in investment banking and asset management.

However, experience from other sectors, such as business school rankings, suggests there is a danger that the tail will start to wag the dog. League tables may encourage firms to offer only services whose value can be easily quantified and to avoid undertaking work where the outcome is uncertain.

Scenario 2: living in a low-margin world

Although most firms, especially those that retain a partnership structure, play their operational cards close to their chests, it is clear that a combination of fierce competition and a more sophisticated client base have put pressure on prices. At the same time, professional services firms have been spending more: competing to attract high-calibre employees; investing in global infrastructure; and fending off competitors through expensive brand building.

These trends will continue, so success in the future for a professional services firm will mean adapting to this new, low-margin world by cutting costs, selling more, charging differently or doing less:

- **Cutting costs.** Around two-thirds of the costs of a typical professional services firm are people-related. Firms can opt to pay less, and many during the recent recession have opted to do this. This is not a sustainable strategy, however, as it might mean losing talented people to higher-paying competitors. Even during economic downturns, firms see themselves as competing in the "war for talent". A better strategy is to use fewer people. The professional services industry was the last bastion of manual processes. Ironically, when consulting firms were making millions of dollars implementing new IT systems for their clients, their own back-office and front-office processes were in a woeful state. Professional services firms argue that their work depends on face-to-face contact and bespoke, almost hand-crafted services, and most have stuck to their offices which, although expensive, are conveniently located near to their clients. But while maintaining face-to-face contact, firms also need to cut costs. Many have moved some of their functions, usually back-office processes, to low-cost locations overseas, but as margins narrow, some front-office services may also be done remotely or even automated. This will trigger a debate about what a professional service is. For example, is an audit a process of checking data (which could be automated) or an opinion from an auditor (which could not)? It may also open up the market to new, low-cost, high-volume competitors, as has happened in some legal services.

◩ **Selling more.** Falling demand in many markets has not prevented many professional services firms from continuing to pursue growth. Some have narrowed the focus of their sales activities to an unprecedented degree; some have recruited dedicated sales teams to maintain momentum in critical markets; others have used publications, direct mailing, events and multimedia websites as channels to market.

◩ **Charging differently.** More firms will switch to being paid either on a fixed-price basis or according to the value delivered. As discussed in Chapter 16, the proportion of fees paid on a performance-related basis is low for both good and bad reasons. The main reason is that many professional services are hard to value. Firms' and clients' efforts to measure value may help, but firms are likely to focus more on services that are easier to measure.

◩ **Doing less.** Limited budgets and a shift towards tried-and-tested services will make it harder to justify developing new tools and techniques. One effect will be greater commoditisation (see

Scenario 3), but it will also constrain future growth and may pave the way for new entrants bringing in innovative business models, perhaps from other sectors. Astute professional services firms may decide that a better approach would be to become talent spotters, identifying and nurturing innovative ideas developed in client organisations, at business schools, and so on.

Scenario 3: commoditisation

Lower margins are one of several signs of commoditisation already observable in some markets for professional services: prices are falling, and clients complain that they can see no difference between suppliers and that there is nothing new in what they are offering. None of this is new: commoditisation has always snapped at the heels of professional advisers. Interest in new tools and services grows, then wanes as clients learn how to apply them and become reluctant to pay outside advisers to do so on their behalf. Twenty years ago building new-fangled spread-sheets was an important source of revenue for many strategy consulting firms, something that seems almost unbelievable today. The problem is that the "rate" of commoditisation appears to be increasing.

In 2001, an article by four Louisiana-based academics, Paula Carson, Patricia Lanier, Kerry Carson and Brandi N. Guidry, "Clearing a path through the management fashion jungle: some preliminary trailblazing", argued that management fads had increasingly short shelf-lives. Using the number of academic articles produced and the point at which their production peaked (not a perfect measure, but still a useful indicator), Carson and her colleagues calculated that PERT (programme evaluation and review technique) diagrams, which first made an appearance in the 1950s, had a long, shallow curve. There were almost 15 years between the first articles being published and the peak of activity, and the average number of articles being published in the peak years was 44. By contrast, interest in business process re-engineering, one of the most popular management tools of the 1990s, lasted a mere three years, but, at the height of its popularity, this subject generated 130 articles. "Slow-burn" services have been replaced by ones that burn brighter but for a shorter period of time.

The reasons for this trend are not clear. The internet has made it easier for organisations to gather their own information, identify tools and techniques that may help them, and connect with other organisations that may have dealt with similar issues. For example, a company considering entering a new country will be able to find macroeconomic data on prospects for growth, research on how consumers behave and statistics on competitors relatively quickly and easily. In the past, it might have taken a strategy consultancy several weeks to assemble such information. More managers have some type of professional qualification, so the gap between their knowledge and that of their external advisers is shrinking. In 1977, ten years after it had been set up, the Association of MBAs had about 2,000 members; today it has over 9,000.

Organisations with better-qualified staff and greater access to information will put pressure on professional services firms to differentiate their expertise by investing in proprietary methodologies and sources of data. "Thought leadership", the publication of articles and reports on specific issues, has become one way in which firms do this (the top 30 professional services firms list more than 15,000 on their websites). However, their ability to improve the quality of their research and develop more innovative ideas may be compromised in the future. Lack of differentiation between professional services firms and their clients puts pressure on prices, reducing the amount of money to invest in increasing that differentiation in the future.

Scenario 4: changing organisational models

The traditional pyramid structure of a professional services firm will be harder to sustain in future if clients, as they are likely to do, cherry-pick the people they want at the price they are prepared to pay – what people in the consulting industry call "body-shopping". Conventional forms of body-shopping put the onus of work and responsibility on clients: they have to identify the right people and make sure they can work effectively together. Although this gives them a wider range of views, it has not proved easy to build high-performing teams from competing firms. In the new approach to "multisourcing", the supplier will be expected to pull in specialist services from other sources rather than staffing projects with its own people. For some firms, the skills of finding and combining resources will become a core competence, giving them a competitive advantage over rivals which struggle – financially, organisationally and culturally – with this type of inclusive approach.

The pyramid-shaped firm may be reaching the end of its life in other ways. For clients wanting access to experts with specialised skills in specific fields, firms where the bottom of the pyramid has become stretched have never been suitable. Because most professional services firms make more money from their junior staff than from their senior ones, and because they need their senior people to be drumming up new business, more work has been done by junior staff. For the professional services industry, the pyramid model is unwieldy and a poor base from which to diversify. Because so much hangs on the ratio of junior to senior staff, it generally becomes a series of vertical "silos" or fiefdoms focused on individual partners.

Other options are to stay small, focusing on a particular area, and form alliances with other firms specialising in different fields; to hire staff on a short-term or associate basis; or to adopt a more conventional corporate structure with larger pools of people who can be moved from one project to another. Given the diverse nature of professional services, none of the options are perfect; but firms will continue to experiment with different structures for the foreseeable future.

The implications for purchasing

For purchasing teams, the differences between professional services firms will become clearer:

- **Advice versus implementation.** Professional services firms largely give advice. A consulting company provides recommendations and may support in some way the delivery of a new strategy, but it is not responsible for its entire implementation. A law firm may help a client negotiate an acquisition, but the final decision rests with the client. However, economic incentives, industry structures and human nature make the advice–implementation distinction hard to maintain. The pressures outlined above may force firms to throw their hat into just one ring: will they become advisers working on small, high-margin projects; or high-volume, low-margin delivery machines?
- **Large versus small.** Consolidation among mid-tier players and the increasing use of preferred supplier lists (which focus expenditure on a small number of firms) will mean greater polarisation. Only a few large firms will have the scale, global reach and brand recognition to handle the largest projects. To survive, the plethora of small firms will have to become even more specialised, and although their lower fee rates will make them attractive, clients will struggle to find them and find it hard to judge their quality.
- **Leaders versus followers.** Although commoditisation will increase the need for innovation, lower margins will limit firms' capacity to invest. Professional services firms will have to choose between the two: some will use all their spare capacity to identify

and develop new ideas, tools and services; others will eschew such high-risk, costly speculation in favour of making the most of their cash-generating services, even if these are less profitable.

- **Volume versus value.** Some firms will focus on volume, industrialising their services so they can guarantee the benefits and drive down the costs of delivery. Others will remain more traditional "craft-based" firms, offering a bespoke service at a higher margin. However, most sizeable firms will find themselves trapped in the middle, offering a combination of volume and value in different parts of their business.

- **Brands versus factories.** Financial services institutions have already started to divide into two groups: those with the better-known brands focus their resources on dealing with consumers and marketing; those whose core competencies lie in developing new products become the "factories" that serve the market. This could happen in professional services, especially if multisourcing becomes widespread. Instead of assuming they have to "own" all aspects of delivery, professional services firms may decide that some work is better done by lesser-known, specialist firms – the factories in this analogy.

- **Skills versus outcomes.** There may be a fundamental change in what organisations think they are buying and what professional services firms think they are selling. In the past, this was almost always skills – firms were offering experts in particular fields – and it remains true today, even among the largest professional services firms. There is nothing intrinsically wrong with this model, except where a firm fails to recognise that there is another approach. In future some firms will start to focus on packaged services or outcomes: clients will be buying the output, not the inputs. Choosing between these two models will depend on the service sought: an individual to plug a temporary gap or a specific result.

Whichever scenario comes to pass, successful procurement teams will be those that keep their finger on the market pulse and are prepared to adapt their approach to the changing shape of the professional services sector. Their market understanding and awareness will be crucial, enabling them to maintain their credibility with internal stakeholders and deliver strong purchasing performance.

Index